ORPHANHOOD

a feeling of being forsaken

María Gabriela González Mendoza

Orphanhood
A Feeling of Being Forsaken

María Gabriela González Mendoza
info@coronadejusticia.com
www.coronadejusticia.com

@coronadejusticiaoficial

WhatsApp: +57 316 399 1220

Editor: Amy Davis
Spanish Edition: Luis Enrique Ramos
Spanish Designer: Pahola Andrea Ramos Barbour
English translation: Perla Cabrera Mora; Nadia K. Mora.

ISBN: 978-958-49-4981-3
E-Book ISBN: 978-958-49-4991-2

Printed in Colombia by Editorial Buena Semilla.

Table of Contents

Acknowledgments 5
Dedication 7
Prologue I 9
Prologue II 13
My Testimony 15
Introduction 31

CHAPTER 1
Fatherhood and
Orphanhood (Identity) 35

Prayer to receive God's Fatherhood
and Identity (Orphanhood) 87

CHAPTER 2
Fatherhood and
Love (Fear) 89

Prayer to receive God's
Fatherhood and Love (Fear) 115

CHAPTER 3
Fatherhood and
Grace (Condemnation/Works) 119

Prayer to receive God's Fatherhood
and Grace (Condemnation/Works) 147

CHAPTER 4
Fatherhood and
Worship (Soul tie/Lies) 149

Prayer to receive God's Fatherhood
and to Worship Him (Soul tie/Lies) 163

CHAPTER 5
Fatherhood and
Freedom (Slavery) 165

Prayer to receive God's
Fatherhood and Freedom (Slavery) 197

CHAPTER 6
Fatherhood and
Power (Intimidation) 199

Prayer to receive God's
Fatherhood and Power (Intimidation) 219

CHAPTER 7
Fatherhood and
Glory (Hypocrisy) 221

Prayer to receive God's
Fatherhood and Glory (Hypocrisy) 259

First Testimony: From Orphanhood to
Having the Identity of Being A Child of God 261

Second Testimony: From Heartbreak
to the Father´s Perfect Love 267

Third Testimony: From Slavery to the
Freedom of Being a Child of God 271

Conclusion 279

Acknowledgments

I want to thank the heavenly Father for sending Jesus Christ. I want to thank Christ for being obedient unto death. I want to thank the Holy Spirit for adopting all of the orphans.

I thank my mother Silvia Esther Mendoza Forero for carrying me in her womb and giving me life. Thank you for never ceasing to cry out, for your unbreakable strength, for your ability to move forward amidst pain. Thank you for every prayer you made for me, they changed the course of my life. Thank you for always believing in what God has given me, for being my faithful friend, my greatest witness, and my confidant. Thank you. I love you.

"...Blessed is the womb that bore You, and the breasts which nursed You!" (Luke 11:27).

I want to thank Pastor Yrazema Lilia Rojas de Gómez. Thank you for being an instrument of God in my life and letting God use you so that the Son of God could deliver me from orphanhood. Thank you for every early morning you patiently listened to the deep brokenness of my confused heart. I love you.

I want to thank Luisa Cristina Pérez de Torres for every prayer, teaching, and exhortation; and for every hug with which you sweetly dried my tears. Thank you for showing me what it means to be strong and to overcome. Thank you for prophetically guiding me every step of the way leading up to this book. I love you.

I want to thank Virginia Elena Martín de Naranjo. Thank you because, through your example, I came to know what a godly, loving, prudent woman looks like. Thank you for guiding me with all the knowledge God has given you of the Sacred Scriptures, and thanks for answering all of my questions. I love you.

Dedication

There he was; a dreamer, challenger of the future. Intelligent, passionate, and expectant of life ahead. He was a lawyer, great in his time, prominent and with eyes that sparkled, though full of tears. He was sensitive but outstanding, though he lacked affection he was willing to give it. His heart, though wounded, was always strong. He made many mistakes but also had great successes. The man I honored until the last day of his life and of whom I was always proud. He understood my heart and was the one waiting for me when I was born, surprised by how much we looked alike. He loved me from the very first day. He was the one who carried me in his arms when I fell asleep and carried me to bed even though he knew I was actually awake.

That man, Arquímedes Enrique González Fernández (1944-2004), was my beloved father, my teacher, and the love of my life. His love was like a permanent ink stamp imprinted on my heart. His teachings are etched in my blood in an unremovable way. He was the one from whom I inherited my deep love for books. To this passionate, romantic, and dreamy man, I dedicate this, my first work: Orphanhood.

I thank God for the father who begot me.

"...for love will cover a multitude of sins" (1 Peter 4:8b).

Prologue I

The feeling of orphanhood is what I experienced the night I found out my beloved parents had died. I said to myself, "I'm an orphan now, my parents are gone". The emptiness, loneliness, and abandonment I felt were very intense. Along with the lack of protection, affection, and love that only our parents could give. However, it was very beautiful to hear the healing voice of the Holy Spirit. He enlightened my understanding of His Word and told me that I was not an orphan and that He was with me.

"When my father and my mother forsake me, then the Lord will take care of me" (Psalm 27:10).

I definitely believe that the enemy of our lives roams the earth producing the evil feeling of orphanhood. He screams from hell itself that we are alone, that we are orphans, that no one will come to rescue us, and that we deserve to be rejected by God. He screams that we must die in orphanhood, insecurity, and ignoring who we are for God, for those around us, and also for ourselves. However, because of our heavenly Father's love that is given to us through His Holy Spirit, He always comes to our rescue with His mighty Word; just like He did for the Apostle Paul:

"O wretched man that I am! Who will deliver me from this body of death? I thank God—through Jesus Christ our Lord! So then, with the mind I myself serve the law of God, but with the flesh the law of sin" (Romans 7:24-25).

I am immensely grateful to God for our sister María Gabriela González Mendoza, who with great zeal, dedication, and diligence has dedicated herself to researching this issue. She has allowed God, our heavenly Father, to show her the long-awaited solution to the orphanhood that is present in the world, and surprisingly in the Body of Christ, as well. That solution is the fatherhood of our God.

You will laugh, cry and surrender to the Divine fatherhood as you read this book. You will enjoy how she intertwines her testimonies and personal experiences. But above all, you will experience complete freedom from orphanhood by delving into the biblical principles that María Gabriela exposes and connects to the Word about identity, love, grace, worship, freedom, power, and finally, glory.

Our sister María Gabriela masterfully links biblical pearls that bring healing to all ages and cultures. She does this through what God has allowed her to see and understand about the fatherhood that eradicates the torment of orphanhood in people who still have not forgiven their parents, loved ones, and friends who caused them pain in the past.

This book is like a hidden treasure that motivates us to fall in love with the heavenly Father more and more because of the rights He gave us through our Lord Jesus Christ.

I have great respect and admiration for my sister María Gabriela and her ministry; especially because of her sensitivity and readiness to obey God's voice. Just like King David went from taking care of his father's sheep and emerged into being the King of Israel, in this fantastic book about how to confront and eradicate orphanhood, María Gabriela emerges with a healing, liberating, and indispensable message for our hurting society.

I am sure that just like me, you will also go deeper and experience the truths embodied in this book on a personal level. There's no doubt that you will be ministered to and that your relationship with your heavenly Father will be enriched.

Nowadays, we see many people suffering from orphanhood and feeling disconnected from life and from God because they are far from the identity and beautiful fatherhood that Jesus models for us. Jesus spoke of the Father in the Gospels 252 times and twice in the book of Acts; each verse shows a different facet of His great love, but above all, of His responsibility to never abandon us.

"And I will pray to the Father, and He will give you another Helper, that He may abide with you forever—I will not leave you orphans; I will come to you. But the Helper, the Holy Spirit, whom the Father will send in My name, He will teach you all things, and bring to your remembrance all things that I said to you" (John 14:16, 18, 26).

My dear sister María Gabriela, thank you very much for allowing the Father to enlighten your eyes to see that where orphanhood abounded, FATHERHOOD ABOUNDED EVEN MORE!

Juan Carlos Jiménez Herrera
Senior Pastor
Casa de Celebración (House of Celebration)
Houston, TX.

Prologue II

During the time we´ve been working in the inner healing ministry, God has taught us to recognize and understand the reasons why His children remain in captivity. Among these causes was the lack of identity; not understanding who people are as new creatures in Christ Jesus our Lord.

María Gabriela, the author of this book, is a daughter of God. Though she is young, because of what she has lived and the days she's spent surrendered to God in absolute devotion and humility, she fully understood this reality and embraced it in such a way that God has led her even deeper.

I know that what God has revealed to her regarding this truth will shake many people to their core. Orphanhood helps us understand the need for an identity in Christ to thereby find our inner healing and freedom from bitterness and pain.

I know that throughout these pages, the reader will go deeper into the healing and freedom he needs, as he encounters the truth of our Eternal Father as the only true God. María Gabriela certifies it in the content of this book: "Identity gives you the courage to face whatever comes your way. Know that the Father loves you and that He has forgiven you. He has washed your filth with the blood of His beloved Son, His grace has redeemed you, and He has justified you with His holiness". In addition, it will allow you to enter His presence and present yourself before Him as an approved worker who has no reason to be ashamed.

Virginia Elena Martín de Naranjo

My Testimony

I grew up in a dysfunctional family made up of my father, mother, and six sisters. My parents had a son I never met because he died before I was born. I am number seven in my family. My older sisters are daughters of another father, which makes my family the combination of two broken homes. My parents had children in their previous marriages, so my father and mother began to build their lives and new family on everyone's pain.

As a little girl, I would sit and dream, imagine, and think about the future, believing that I could achieve anything. In my mind, I never felt limited, I felt free to plan, design, and create.

My father was a lawyer and author of legal works; a professional who defined himself as a "winner of cases." He was intelligent, a dreamer, intellectual, and caring. But he was also depressed and emotionally unstable. My mother is a beautiful woman, very capable, with great social intelligence, and unshakable inner strength. However, she was prey to fear and rejection, so she wasn't the typical mom who hugged us or gave us words of affirmation.

My relationship with my sisters was awful. If I could define what they were like to me with one word it would be: *persecutors*. My dad was very sweet and loving; he never grew tired of kissing my hands and face in a delicate and tender way. He used to sit me on his lap and call me his little darling. That's what it was like for me while I lived with him until I was nine years old; there was a big distinction between my sisters and me. For example, he wouldn't take me to school if I asked him to stay home because I was sleepy, or sometimes he would let me tag along on a work trip. To him, I was his pretty little girl, but he was rigid towards my sisters and rejected them, showing no emotion or affection. Evidently, God does not approve of this kind of treatment called favoritism.

The fact is that´s why I became the target of my sisters´ jealousy and envy, it's why they treated me badly when he was away. My mother treated me well because she was one of those women who were emotionally dependent on men and did whatever he wanted as long as he was around. I also look like him physically, he had white skin and slightly light eyes while my mother has a darker skin tone. All of these things summed up the rivalry between my sisters and me.

When my sisters played together they didn't include me, which resulted in my emotional ups and downs. I was, as the Bible says, double-minded. When my dad was around I felt loved and happy, but when he was absent I felt sad and rejected, stuck between a rock and a hard place.

But when I was nine years old, my dad left us to start a third family, causing great pain with his departure. This time we were the victims; my sisters, my mother, and I were the ones left alone. One day, they took us out of school and we moved to a new city. There was a client from another part of the country, outside of the capital, who offered my father a case to defend. I was in third grade at the time and remember how sad I was to leave my friends.

My parents set up a law firm to handle this case. He hired a secretary who was 27 years younger than him, with whom he started a romantic relationship. Then, one day he told my mom they needed to turn in the apartment we had rented while we settled in that city. He said we would be moving to another apartment. She packed up our belongings and we went to the town square where he told us to wait for him. We were there from morning until 12 at night, and he never came back for us. I remember my younger sister telling my mother, "I'm sleepy!", "I am hungry!", "Why are we here?" Imagine this woman, a foreigner with only a third-grade education and no residency documents to work. On top of all that, she was sitting with all of us girls in the middle of a city, late at night where she didn't know anyone. No family or money to move on.

The way my mother handled this situation shows what she's made of. I remember we walked to the hotel that was across the street. My mom took out some gold jewelry from her purse and offered them to the manager as collateral, asking him to please let us spend the night and that in the morning she would pay for the room. When the man looked at us, I suppose he was moved by compassion. He allowed us to stay the night without accepting the jewelry. After we were settled in, he brought us a bag of sweet bread and two liters of milk. I remember my little sister eating desperately because she had been hungry for so long. It was one of the saddest and most confusing days of my life. The man I loved, my protector, had left us for reasons I didn't understand at that age. A deep pain came over me, but I watched in silence what was happening around me. In the following days, we moved to a dangerous and ugly neighborhood where they rented rooms for students. The owner would give my mom the water where she boiled the meat in, so that we could make something to eat.

My sisters' lives and mine changed completely. I remember thinking: *"What happened?"*, *"Where is my dad?"*, *"Doesn't he care about us?"*, *"Doesn't he love us?"*, *"Why did he abandon us?"* I saw my mother carry the weight of this great burden; we had no money, no friends, no family, and she had no one to help her. I remember how she would sit on the stairs to cry and how quickly she lost weight. But every day she went out to look for opportunities to move on. This kind of situation deeply hurts and impacts a child's emotional system. Personally, it was very intense because I was convinced that my father loved me, but all I could feel was a deep loneliness. My sisters mistreated me and reproached me because of him, they'd tell me he had always been a bad person and other mean things like that.

That was their opinion of him, which I am able to understand today. He had treated them badly but gave me special treatment. Though he had left us, in my heart, I refused to feel resentment because the love he had given me was so deeply rooted in my heart. I still loved him and my whole being wanted to justify him; I thought there had to be an explanation for everything that had happened. After that, I became a very quiet and lonely person. I lived feeling like someone was waiting for my situation to change to seize the opportunity to get back at me.

On the other hand, my mother became bitter, abusive and offensive. She reproached me by telling me that I looked just like him and took me to places where women spoke badly of my father, laughing and mocking him. It upset me because they were making fun of the most important person in the world for a girl my age. My mother took her anger out on me and would tell me that if I loved him so much I should just go with him. She said that all the love he had given me wouldn't pay for my school. There was constant friction between my mother and I. This mistreatment motivated my sisters to make fun of me and bully me even more, which made me insecure and depressed, and I just wanted to die. So when I was 10 years old, I locked myself in the bathroom and took a large number of pills. I had no source of love, I was unhappy, and I couldn't find a reason to live. The fact that there were so many of them against me, and they all agreed with one another made me feel alone and unprotected. One of my sisters was very aggressive and hit me when my mom was at work. I felt nobody was there for me, nobody cared, and there was nobody to defend me. I felt empty and low on love. They all hated my dad and they wanted me to hate him too. But I refused, not knowing the great purpose God had with all of it.

Despite all of this, I continued to dream. At just 10 years old, I´d say things like, *"I am going to be a lawyer!"*, and, *"I see myself walking in the streets of London wearing a long black coat!"* My sisters made fun of me and one, who was especially annoyed by my statements, told me, "Understand that we are poor; you´re an orphan with holes in her shoes." She'd say other things like that, but I didn't pay any attention to her. I would just respond that I was not an orphan.

Time passed and by the time I was 17 years old, adolescence had come accompanied by rebellion. All the seeds of abuse that my mother had sown in me with her insults and mockery, as well as my sisters´ mistreatment, began to surface. I was no longer quiet and submissive, I became irreverent. I was so hurt and empty that I became offensive and revengeful, with a big need to be approved and loved.

I remember the first time I saw my father again was when I was 17 years old. I loved him then as I always had and I just wanted to run into his arms. It was as if time had not passed and the pain was not caused. He was the same as I had remembered; he gave me so many kisses, hugs and was just as kind. But now he was older, sad, and had teary eyes full of remorse. He also faced the effects of a stroke which prevented movement from his hand to his foot on the entire left part of his body. He had a motor and language disability and spoke like a baby learning to talk. The doctors said he needed to stimulate his brain so he could learn to speak again. I used to call him to talk, but all I heard was my dad crying on the other side of the line. Seeing him like this made me very sad because he was no longer the man I remembered. He wasn't strong and elegantly dressed, he was shriveled up and sick. During that season, I had the opportunity to spend a lot of time with him. He didn't have money, food, or anything really. At the time, I worked at Subway, so every day I´d take him the food they gave me at work, buy his medicine, and do everything I could for him. I couldn't give him much at 17, but I constantly told him I loved him and that I had never judged him. Never did I demand anything from him either; I think he judged himself for what he had done. His condition was very difficult, but the love he was receiving motivated him so much that he began to write his last book. I accompanied him to the courtrooms and would hear him say, *"This is my daughter. She is going to be a lawyer."* His words became my identity.

When I was 18, my mother told me she was ill, had lots of debt, and that we couldn't stay in the apartment we were living in. So I began to take on life with the backpack she'd given me and the autonomy over myself to decide what to do. I was alone, penniless, and at a very crucial age. The most difficult thing was trying to face my life with the echo of the words my sisters had planted in my heart. I was also very sad because of the abuse, rejection, and lack of protection; I cried every day. From time to time, I could at least see my father and although he couldn't offer me any help, it gave me a little bit of hope.

At the age of 19, after having recovered my relationship with my father two years prior, he died due to a fulminating heart attack. When they called me to break the news, I just kept thinking, *"This can't be true."* But the day came when they flew him to the city where he was going to be buried. My paternal grandmother, his first wife, and his first children lived there, so from my family, it was just my older sister and I at the funeral. I remember it was a horrible, rainy day. My two older brothers from my dad›s side had to lift me up, each one taking me by an arm because I didn't have the strength to get up to see my dad. They accompanied me and put my arms on the glass of the coffin so I could hold myself up. My dad's skin was green... and once again something inside me broke that day. I cried until the veins in my eyes were marked on my eyelids. My older sister had great resentment against my father. When she heard me crying in the room, she knocked on the door saying, "Shut up, stop crying!" She didn't understand what I was feeling. I had lost the only person on this earth that had treated me with love. Now, I was completely alone. When he was alive, I was at least comforted by having him around. But I couldn't take refuge in her, even though she was my sister from the same father and the same mother, it was like being there with an enemy. When it came time to bury him and shovels of sand were thrown over the coffin, I shouted, *"You left me alone! You left me!"*

I said it over and over again. I sat down to cry as they poured sand on him because my legs were too weak for me to stand. One of my father›s sisters told me, *"Jump in if you want."* Maybe she said it to encourage me, but she had no idea the effect those words had on me. That day, in my heart I threw myself into that hole of death. That was the saddest and darkest day of all my life. I stayed in the city for almost three months in my cousin´s house crying and barely eating. I just kept thinking, *"What am I going to do? Where am I going to go?"*

But the most predominant feelings were, *"I´m alone"*, *"Nobody loves Me"*, *"I have no one."* Although sometimes we think that our childhood is irrelevant to the development of our life, that is not really the case. Our childhood marks the path we will walk for the rest of our existence. This season shapes our character and the way we face difficulties. All of these impacts remain deep within us and shape who we become. Never having a place of refuge and arms to hug us when we feel sad makes us insecure, arrogant, proud, and haughty. It develops in us a feeling of superiority or inferiority and robs us of our strength to take on life.

After all of this suffering, with great effort, I began to study law and move on with my life. I became even more depressed and cried every day while looking to men to give me the love I didn't have. I wanted to be accepted by them and looked for protection and help in every one of them. But because I was so hurt, I lived with many insecurities.

I had been in a relationship for six years, and when he asked me to marry him I said yes. Our relationship was very problematic, so I doubted my decision. I harbored in my heart the longing to have a beautiful family. The kind of family that is your safe place, where no one can hurt you. The wedding was going to be in a five-star hotel with lots of guests; the invitations had been sent out and everything was ready for the big day. But 15 days before the wedding, I heard a voice inside me telling me, "Don't get married, I'm not in it." This was a big deal, I couldn´t just say, "You know what? I don't want to get married anymore." But I listened to the inner voice. Despite all of the conflict, I would have to face my boyfriend and everyone we had hired, so I called it off. As you can imagine, he never wanted to speak to me again and I understood why, but I was calm. Two months later, he posted a picture with another girl and I literally felt the ground shake beneath me. I knew I didn›t want to marry him because of all the conflicts we had, but I still loved him, or at least that›s what I thought. At that moment, the traumas, insecurities, wounds, conflicts, and everything I had bottled up inside came out. It all surfaced and I thought, *"This is too much, I won't be able to overcome this."* And even if I believed we could solve our problems, the voice I heard was the voice of God. We didn›t get married, we never got back together, and I never saw that man again. That is where my walk with the Lord began.

The day I saw that picture, I was crying while driving my car, thinking about how Christian people listened to a different kind of music. Something inside me prompted me to look for worship music, but I didn't know where to find it. I decided to go to a Christian church around seven in the morning and walked in on an intercession group. I thought they would pray for me and help me, but that's not what happened. Those prayer times in the church are for people who intercede. So when I walked in, they gave me a token to pray. When it was my turn in the prayer circle I just started to cry. I felt out of place and explained I couldn´t intercede for anyone because I didn't know how to pray. Two of the leaders accompanied me out of the room and prayed for me at the end of the meeting. They told me God had a purpose for me and that is why He had led me there, but none of that made sense to me at that time. One of them gave me her phone number and told me to call her if I needed anything. I left but around four in the afternoon that same day, the pain became unbearable. I didn't know what to do, and for the first time, I called on the name of Jesus, saying, *"Jesus, I heard that You are a friend. If You really exist, help me today because if not, I am going to die."*

It wasn't something I said lightly. I think the Lord knows when we've reached our limit. If something wouldn't have happened that day, I would have taken my life away. I wanted to find a place that sold worship music, and I remembered that the church leader had given me her number. So I called her and said, *"Hi, I'm the one who went to church today. I am feeling very discouraged, could you pray for me?"* She answered, *"I'm not just going to pray for you, I want to go visit you. Where do you live?"*

This precious daughter of God came to my home with a worship CD, a book on prayer, and a folder with a 21-day fasting program. At that moment I felt as if Jesus was telling me, *"I exist and I am here through her."* So I assumed that it was directly Him who wanted me to do that fast, and it really was! I was so broken that I fasted for 21 days; I cried, read the

Word of God, and lost 26 pounds. My days became like a Christian movie; I'd sit on my couch in the living room of my house to read the Bible when the sun was coming up and when night fell I was still there reading the Holy Scriptures. For the first time in my life, I didn't leave my house, work, watch TV, talk to anyone, or surf the Internet. And not just for the 21 days of the fast, but for two years. It was truly amazing because the gospel began to be revealed to me and I started having dreams that convinced me of sin, judgment, and righteousness. I knew I needed God's forgiveness. I felt sinful and because I had never heard of Him, I had lived in a worldly way without the knowledge of God and His commandments. Sin was the reason for my brokenness. I remember sitting on the floor for hours singing a worship song called, *"Al estar ante Ti" (To Be Before You)* by Alejandro del Bosque. I felt like a leper in front of the Lord and every day I prayed to Him, *"Lord, if You want You can cleanse me"*.

There was a wonderful pastor who helped me and led my healing process. When I met her, I felt I had finally found someone who understood what I was feeling. I began to see her every Friday after that. She has an impressive gift of discernment, it was like she could hear my thoughts.

One day I was driving around town. Though I already knew the Lord, I was sad and cried as I drove. I had horrible emotional breakdowns that made me want to find my ex-boyfriend, the one I was going to marry. I thought he was the only one who could help me because he had been my best friend. Even though it had been two years since I ended the relationship, I wanted to run back to him, but obviously, he didn't want to talk to me. I didn't know what to do, but the Holy Spirit taught me that if you ask your soul how it feels, it will tell you where it's been taken captive, because out of the abundance of the heart the mouth speaks. So just like when King David asked his soul, *"Why so downcast, my soul, why so troubled within me?"* I asked my soul, "*What's the matter? How do you feel?"*

And at that moment I screamed out, *"I feel like an orphan!"* When I heard that answer, I stayed quiet, wiped my tears and thought, *"What does this mean? What do you mean orphan?"* This word didn›t make sense to me. I never thought of myself as an orphan. I thought orphans were children in orphanages without parents, but I had parents.

That same day I had to go to the pastor's house and the Lord used her discernment to bring deliverance in a surprising way. I decided to fast so I could be ready to share what the Holy Spirit had done. But before I could start telling her, she said, "*The Holy Spirit showed me that you have a spirit of orphanhood."* I was speechless. My mother was with me and she knew it was true because of what had happened in the car just a few hours before. That day we prayed and my spiritual eyes were opened.

I saw myself wearing a white robe in a dark stone room, similar to a cell. I was kneeling on the bed with my shoes off. There was a closed gate and two people who looked like guards were standing in front of it. The pastor told me to put my feet on the ground. But it was moldy and I didn't want to touch it so I started kicking my feet around. It was as if my soul woke up because of the place I was in and the trauma intensified. I could feel the anguish; meanwhile, she insisted, *"Put your feet on the ground, don't worry about your shoes because when you get out of here you'll have lots of shoes."* While all this was happening, what impressed me the most, apart from the spiritual vision, was that the pastor was seeing the same thing as me. We were both seeing the same thing in the same spiritual dimension.

I started to scream but she said, *"Don't worry, you don't have to do anything, let Jesus do it."* She began to sing and call out to Jesus. I saw Him come and stand in front of the fence. The light was really the only thing I could see, and then the gate opened. He carried me and we went up the stairs of the cell. They were damp and moldy, but as He went up they became white and new. When we reached the top, that dark place disappeared and I saw that we were in a very high place without a roof, where the only thing we could see was light. That same day the teaching at the pastor's house was about this verse, *"I am the way, and the truth, and the life; no one comes to the Father, except through Me."* I had literally just seen it with my spiritual eyes! That day this Scripture became as real as flesh and bone to me. Time went on and I continued my process.

One night, I was getting ready to go to bed and knelt down to pray. It was a simple prayer, like the one you pray before going to sleep. But suddenly, a presence fell on my shoulders and pushed me down. I started to cry and kept saying, *"Father, Father, I´m sorry Father, You are my Father; forgive me, forgive me."* I was on the ground crying without stopping for a few minutes because the weight of His presence prevented me from lifting my head. By then, I already had a relationship with God, I read His Word every day, and was completely isolated from the world. So I asked the Lord, *"What is this?"*, and He answered me clearly, *"You are receiving the spirit of adoption."* That day, I didn´t imagine what this experience would mean or the impact it would have on me.

This revelation changed my life forever. He healed my wounds and forever transformed my relationship with my mom and my sisters, who came to know Christ and now lovingly serve Him. This revelation has also changed the lives of many people. One day, I had a dream where the Lord told me to write. Time later, a prophetess from the church I was attending told me that God had called me to write. I had kept the dream hidden in my heart and hadn't told anyone, so I confirmed that her prophecy came from God. That is why, despite not being a theologian or a writer, I was inspired to share this message so that many souls could be freed from orphanhood through the revelation that the spirit of adoption has ministered to my life.

Introduction

The word "*family*" comes from the Greek term "*patria*"[1], which is derived from the word "*pater*", which means "*father*"[2]. In Ephesians 3:14-15, the apostle Paul states:

"*For this reason I bow my knees to the Father of our Lord Jesus Christ, from whom the whole family in heaven and earth is named*".

---

1 Spanish Strong Concordance, 3965.

2 Spanish Strong Concordance, 3962.

Paul is referring to the fact that he bent his knees before the Father from whom all fatherhood in heaven and on earth takes its name. Derek Prince says that behind every father is the fatherhood of God. This truth makes it clear that to establish a family there must be a father and without a father, there is no family. This is the reason why so many homes are destroyed. The enemy directly attacks the humanity of men to deconstruct God's design.

Every family's blessing comes from the Father:

"Blessed be the God and Father of our Lord Jesus Christ, who has blessed us with every spiritual blessing in the heavenly places in Christ" (Ephesians 1:3).

Just like the patriarchs blessed their children throughout Scripture, so God the Father blesses His children. Meaning that according to God's design, it is up to men to bless their families. It is the man who imparts the blessing, which means that the blessing comes from the Father.

The greatest void a human being can experience is the absence of a father, and therefore, the absence of a family. And because they do not have it, they incessantly seek to belong to one. Think about it, isn't this what gang members tell teenagers? They promise them a family if they join their groups. The emptiness of not having the shelter of a home at a young age prompts people to find refuge in the streets.

However, God's promise through Jesus Christ says:

"For through Him we both have access by one Spirit to the Father. Now, therefore, you are no longer strangers and foreigners, but fellow citizens with the saints and members of the household (family) of God" (Ephesians 2:18-19 author's emphasis).

The heavenly Father has promised to make you a member of His family and to remove the wounds caused by the pain of forsakenness and homelessness.

"God sets the solitary in families; He brings out those who are bound into prosperity" (Psalm 68:6a).

Without removing a jot or a tittle, in this book, I share all the teachings that God has given me about fatherhood. These things have been entrusted to me after many hours spent on my knees, fasting, and praying in the presence of the Lord. Though I am not a theologian, I urge readers to be like the brothers in Berea. When Paul taught them they welcomed the word with eagerness and a noble heart and examined the Scriptures daily to see if those things were true (Acts 17:11, author's paraphrase).

In this book, you will find hidden treasures and very well-kept secrets in the Word of God. These will heal the wounds caused by the lack of fatherhood that you harbor in your heart. My intention in writing these pages is to bring you to a deep knowledge of the Holy Scriptures and to show you the importance of turning the heart of the fathers towards the children and that of the children towards the fathers. Additionally, I want to guide you on the path beginning with identity that leads to experiencing the glory of God. You will be reconciled with the heavenly Father, discovering the prophetic destiny God has traced for each of His children, as well as the reason for which you were created.

Chapter 1

Fatherhood and Orphanhood

(Identity)

The definition of orphanhood, in the personal sense and in its strictest meaning, is living without parents. As an adjective, it means to be lacking something; a quality or necessary characteristic, especially some kind of protection or help that should be enjoyed.

An orphan is someone who is or feels helpless, abandoned, defenseless, withdrawn, conflicted, self-conscious, and unprotected, or is in a condition of total forsakenness, lacking shelter, and being humiliated.

Orphanhood is not only physical but also spiritual. In this sense, a person can suffer from this condition even having biological parents, stepparents or guardians.

Forsakenness is the result of living in orphanhood since it causes the loss of identity, as well as affliction, anguish, loneliness, depression, distrust, fear, rejection, isolation, condemnation, slavery, lies, hypocrisy, rebellion, anger, and sadness.

The Merriam-Webster Dictionary defines *forsook* as: "to renounce or abandon", another word we can use is *separation*. But how does this separation occur? And who are we separated from? From my approach to the subject and according to biblical truths, one is separated from one's biological or earthly father and from the heavenly Father. Let's see what God's Word says about this:

"*But your iniquities have separated you from your God; and your sins have hidden His face from you, so that He will not hear*" (Isaiah 59:2).

This passage of Scripture reveals that the transgression against God's statutes has produced a separation between Him and man. This separation began with Adam's disobedience. Adam, being the son of God, lost that position because of his sin and thus condemned all mankind to be orphans. This truth is confirmed in the genealogy of Jesus:

"*...the son of Enosh, the son of Seth, the son of Adam, the son of God*" (Luke 3:38).

Forsakenness is a feeling of torment that is present even when one has parents. This is why many people feel like the psalmist:

"*My God, My God, why have You forsaken Me? Why are You so far from helping Me, and from the words of My groan-*

ing? O My God, I cry in the daytime, but You do not hear; and in the night season, and am not silent" (Psalm 22:1-2).

The anguish that King David expressed in these verses is the feeling that orphanhood produces in the human being. It's the thought that God is not listening or responding to the cry of His creation, which is why many people say over and over again: *"If God exists, why did this happen to me?" "Why does He let the world go from bad to worse?"* The answer is the separation caused by sin. The result of this is man´s total independence, disbelief, rebellion, self-sufficiency, and the excessive effort that different religions around the world make to get closer to God by their own means.

What relationship is there between biological fatherhood and heavenly fatherhood? Is God a Father? And if He is, is He an irresponsible Father or does He sustain those He has begotten?

For many people, there is a lot of pain attached to the word *dad*. They often ask themselves, *"Who am I? Where do I come from? Where am I going?"*, especially children who have not had a loving relationship with their parents. When they see other children holding their parents´ hands or hugging them, a pain they cannot explain begins to develop in their hearts. They don´t know that it's related to their identity, only that they are different and feel sad and left behind.

The same happens to children who have been abandoned in orphanages, enrolled in boarding schools, or simply birthed by parents they never met. It also happens to the children of mothers who don´t know who the father is because the baby´s conception was caused by rape or under the influence of intoxicating or hallucinogenic substances. The result is confusion in this child that grows up with a deep wound in their heart. There are also occasions when children are raised by stepparents who are often abusive, indifferent, or good financial providers but do not show affection. The father figure is the one that provides the human being with identity, affirmation, and assurance. If the father has been absent, or present but distant in the relationship, or has been an abuser, the child will grow up to be an insecure person with deep feelings of rejection towards himself and others.

This is called heartbreak because of the lack of love. In many homes, because the father is irresponsible or absent, wounded mothers tell their kids that their dad is no good. They tell them he does not love them or support them. Their complaints aggravate the forsakenness the children feel. God's plan for families is not for children to be raised alone, with stepparents, or in adulterous or divided homes. Yet we know that this is a reality in every country around the world with devastating effects.

The Creator, in addition to being God, is a Father. This truth is found in the Scriptures throughout the ministry of the Lord Jesus Christ on earth. But mankind has only related to God as God, not as their Father. First, because of sin and lack of reconciliation, which comes through faith in the Lord Jesus and our repentance. Secondly, because of the wounds the enemy has caused through their biological father. If the enemy manages to damage the relationship between the child and their father, he also manages to destroy the way they see God, since the father who begot them is a reflection of the heavenly Father. It's very difficult to believe there's a God in heaven who is also a Father who wants to take care of you, protect and provide for you, if the only father you know abused you, abandoned you, or you never knew who he was.

One day, on a trip to Lisbon, I met a young man who was about 28 years old. He was the receptionist at the hotel where I was staying. As I told him about how beautiful God's fatherhood is and how He could take care of him, he said to me, *"Do you think the God you´re talking about is a good Father because He gave you a book and left?"* I was very surprised by his reaction, but I didn´t judge him. When I asked him about his biological father, he said they›d never met because he had left his mother when she was pregnant with him.

The **Creator,** in addition to being God, is the **Father**

At that moment I understood why this gentleman had this perception of God. Every human being is like that. God is a loving and nurturing Father but when you´ve grown up without protection, lacking shelter and affirmation, human logic compares God the Father to your biological father or the stepfather you had. And if the one you´ve seen and had a relationship with never loved you, how can you believe that an invisible God and Father is worried about you? What does the Scripture say about this?

"And as we have borne the image of the man of dust, we shall also bear the image of the heavenly Man" (1 Corinthians 15:49).

The image a person has of their earthly, or biological, father will be the image they have of the heavenly Father.

Throughout my walk with Christ, I have received many teachings about the value of biological fatherhood, after all, the father is who sustains the child. The Creator organized everything in such a way that the one who produces something is obliged to sustain it, just as the earth sustains the trees, the trees the fruits, and the sea the fish. In the same way, God's design is for parents to sustain, affirm, and encourage children, yet we know that God's perfect plan has been under attack from the very beginning of Creation.

How is our identity formed? The first thing we need is to see God as the giver of life because no one can be conceived in a womb without it being God's will. His Word reaffirms this truth in many ways:

"By You I have been upheld from birth; You are He who took me out of my mother's womb. My praise shall be continually of You" (Psalm 71:6).

We see in this Scripture how God sustains life from the womb. He is the Creator, He made you and He is the One who sustains you. Birth is carefully preserved by God, "*... You are He who took me out of my mother's womb...*". Then the questions are: *Why did He bring me out of the womb?* and, *Why does He uphold me?*

You don›t come into the world by human will. Whatever the condition may have been by which you came to this earth, the truth is the Creator was the One who brought you. We all have a purpose; all of creation has a prophetic assignment and destiny. Let›s look at the words of the psalmist David:

"For You formed my inward parts; You covered me in my mother's womb. I will praise You, for I am fearfully and wonderfully made; marvelous are Your works, and that my soul knows very well. My frame was not hidden from You, when I was made in secret, and skillfully wrought in the lowest parts of the earth. Your eyes saw my substance, being yet unformed. And in Your book they all were written, the days fashioned for me, when as yet there were none of them" (Psalm 139:13-16).

Your parents were not the ones who formed you in the womb, it was God. Your parents were just the instruments so that you could go from the heart of God into the earthly realm. Parents are the backbone of this process as well as a representation of God Himself on earth, which is why being separated from them is so painful. No human being can live a blessed life if they have not forgiven their father or mother. This pain and lack of forgiveness take away the person´s vision, causing them to walk in darkness. What do the Scriptures say about this? They contain very strong precepts about this subject:

"Whoever curses his father or his mother, his lamp will be put out in deep darkness" (Proverbs 20:20).

The meaning Scripture gives to the lamp is the revelation of God. Having a broken relationship with our parents is like being in the dark or having our eyes blindfolded because we don´t know who we are, what to do, or what we were born for. There is a veil that prevents us from seeing the purpose for which we came to this earth and what our destiny is, leaving us under a curse. Let's look at what God commands regarding this topic:

"Children, obey your parents in the Lord, for this is right. ´Honor your father and mother´ which is the first commandment with promise: ´that it may be well with you and you may live long on the earth´" (Ephesians 6:1-3).

This passage and the next agree:

"I call heaven and earth as witnesses today against you, that I have set before you life and death, blessing and cursing; therefore choose life, that both you and your descendants may live" (Deuteronomy 30:19).

It is true that as kids we didn't choose abandonment, abuse, and orphanhood, among many experiences that mark our soul with pain. But God, who is just, gives us the opportunity to choose the life we want to live regardless of where we come from or how painful our childhood was. When we choose to forgive and honor them, we choose blessing, life, and to walk with our lamp lit. But if we cling to resentment, to the idea that they do not deserve forgiveness or honor because of the pain they caused, we will be miserable, resentful, and lose our identity. For many years, I´ve seen children who refuse to forgive their parents and judge them by demanding perfection. They do not take their parents´ childhood into consideration, and as time goes by, the behavior they so harshly criticized in their parents becomes their own reality. The man who does not forgive his father for leaving his mother because of adultery ends up doing the same. The woman who does not forgive her mother for her mistreatment ends up mistreating her own children. The one who suffered from their father´s alcoholism, and does not forgive him, does the same when they become an adult. Scripture states:

"Therefore you are inexcusable, O man, whoever you are who judge, for in whatever you judge another you condemn yourself; for you who judge practice the same things" (Romans 2:1).

The surprising thing about the Word of God is that whether you know what's in it or not, it governs the life of all living things and its words are fulfilled with complete sovereignty. The world was constituted on the basis of spiritual and physical laws. For example, if someone jumps off the roof of a building, whether Christian or atheist, they will likely die because of the law of gravity that governs the earth. The same is true for the spiritual law of sowing and reaping; whether you know it or not, you will become what you judge about your parents. The family where we´ve been placed by God is part of His sovereignty.

People who suffer because of rejection from their family, deny their family, and don´t want to live there any longer. When they act like this, they are unaware that they are rejecting God's plan and striking out against a thorn. The heavenly Father did not make a mistake by placing them there; that's the place they need to be in order to fulfill their purpose. So the more time they spend struggling with their family members, the longer it will take them to find the purpose for which God created them. Just as the fruit cannot deny the branch and tree that holds it up, because it would be left alone in the air and fall to the ground, neither can a child deny their parents.

The relationship with an earthly father opens the door to the fatherhood of God. This is the reason why many do not believe in God or simply know Jesus as Lord. They don't go deeper or allow Him to reveal the Father to them, and they fight against the knowledge of fatherhood because of their experiences. In my experience, I believed that God was good because I had a father that loved me. His love inspired me to dream, and although he wasn't perfect, because no one is, I did not judge him. Later, when I learned about the gifts of the Holy Spirit, through them I understood what my father had suffered.

He had been in boarding school from a very young age because in the 1950s wealthy families sent children away to give them a supposedly privileged education. The fact is that I always wondered why he was so depressed. When I was little, there were times I saw him lying in bed with his hands crossed over his chest just thinking and at times even crying. When I was younger and we traveled from one city to another, he listened to sad songs while he was driving, wiping away the tears from his eyes. It always made me sad to see him in that state. When I saw him again, I was 17 years old but he was still the same; always crying, nostalgic, and emotionally unstable. He was looking for the love he never received in women. One day I found the letters he had written to my grandmother while he was at boarding school. At the age of eight, he wrote to her: *"Why don't you come to see me? All the parents come to visit their kids. I am getting good grades and I miss your hugs"*. Imagine how much he suffered locked up in that place from the ages of eight to twelve. The priests mistreated him and the Jesuit education was strict and absolutely devoid of love or any kind of affection. At almost 60 years old, he wrote another letter to his mother that I had the opportunity to read and his words were the same. He was almost 60 years old but the one writing the letter was the same sad boy from boarding school. He always felt guilty and depressed, and he never recovered from the shock that isolation caused him. I believe he died without knowing his pain revolved around that private confinement of his parents´ love and care. He had a father who supported him financially and gave him many privileges, but in his soul, he was an orphan.

What do I want to tell you with all of this? That every parent has their own story, that there are wounds in every heart, and that is why we should not judge others. The father who raped his children may have suffered the same as a child, the abused often becomes the abuser. If you could see their wounds, you could find the reasons that caused yours. If I´ve learned anything from the Word of God, it's that every human being was created in an amazing way:

"Then God said, ´Let Us make man in Our image, according to Our likeness...´" (Genesis 1:26a).

What do you think is the image of God in us? What do you think His likeness is like? You and me!! We were made of His essence. If there is evil in the heart of man it's because there is pain in his past, but it wasn't like that in the beginning:

"Then God saw everything that He had made, and indeed it was very good..." (Genesis 1:31).

Many people ignore why they feel bad or why they hurt others. The answer is simple: there are wounds in their heart. But who do you love more than a child? And who would willingly want to harm their own child? I assure you that if God allowed you to see your parents´ hearts, you would find the wounds that have caused yours.

We´ve already seen God's participation in our life and that of our parents. As for stepparents, they come into a family because of a fractured marriage. Whether it be because one of the parents died and the other parent remarries, or because of divorce.

This unity is not part of the perfect plan God designed for the family because no one can take the place of a biological father or mother. There is a spiritual aspect that goes beyond raising a child; parents transfer their essence to their children, and only they have the authority to sustain what they've conceived. Although there are certainly many men and women who have been exemplary and have assumed a responsibility that was not theirs, in any case, they are not the child's parents. Let's read the following testimony:

One day, in the church where I served, I counseled a young man who had many problems in his finances, his studies, and in designing a plan for his life. I knew it was because of orphanhood, and when I asked him about his father, he told me he had abandoned him at a very young age. He said, however, that he didn't care because he had a stepfather who was better than his dad. He argued that his stepfather supported him and helped his mother, but he judged his biological father for being arrogant and a womanizer. The amazing thing about this case is that this young man was in counseling because of lust, rebellion, vainglory, etc., just like the father who conceived him. According to this young man, his father did not deserve forgiveness and was insignificant to him, since the honor had been granted to his stepfather. The shocking thing is that this young man did not resemble his stepfather, but rather his biological father because he had the exact same bondages.

Certainly, there are many stepparents who deserve recognition. Though we must be grateful for everything, no one can ever take the place of the father who gave you life. Let's see:

"Listen to your father who begot you, and do not despise your mother when she is old" (Proverbs 23:22).

Let´s observe how the Word of God emphasizes that the father who begot you is the one who must be honored as the father. Honoring an uncle, grandfather, stepfather, etc. as a father will cause orphanhood in your heart because you are not being sustained by the person that made it possible for you to be in this world. Why is a male figure other than the biological father honored? In many cases, it's because the father has not had an influence on the child's life and has not been worthy of admiration. Now, is it bad to admire an uncle, grandfather, or stepfather, among others? No, if it's his behavior that is admired. But as long as you persist in honoring others as your father, the emptiness will remain. The word "stepfather" is not in the Word of God, which is why there are many popular sayings that have a negative spiritual background. For example, "The father is not the one who begets, but the one who raises the child." Expressions like this go against the knowledge of God.

They cause pain to a person's heart, resulting in a loss of identity and preventing the person from enjoying heavenly fatherhood. Likewise, when mothers have carried the burden of supporting their children alone, they begin to nullify the father and elevate themselves to a position that is not theirs. Then we say, "She is father and mother." But this is an aberration from the point of view of Creation because it is obviously impossible for a single woman to conceive a child alone. Providing shelter and material things does not make her a father because she was not designed to be the father. In God's Creation, we see that man's nature is different from the woman´s. We have the example of Jesus Christ, who came to earth as a man and presented God the Father in the masculine gender, why? Because man is the image and glory of God on earth and woman is the glory of man:

"For a man indeed ought not to cover his head, since he is the image and glory of God; but woman is the glory of man" (1 Corinthians 11:7).

It was not a woman who died on the cross of Calvary, so the exaltation that single mothers receive, though with great reason, is not entirely harmless. It has a satanic plan to destroy the fatherhood that only comes through men. We might think that they are just popular sayings, but words are spiritual and have a similar effect. Let's see what Scripture says about this:

"You are snared by the words of your mouth; you are taken by the words of your mouth" (Proverbs 6:2).

This passage reveals that we can be in spiritual prisons because of the words we´ve declared. Behind my words is the belief system I formed; I speak what I believe and have in my heart.

Godmothers and godfathers are not biblical either, they were created for pagan ceremonies and rituals. The supposed doctrine or support of this position is that if a child needs a father or mother, the godparents will assume these responsibilities, but the Holy Scriptures establish:

"When my father and my mother forsake me, then the Lord will take care of me" (Psalm 27:10).

This is God's promise to those who have lost their parents.

What happens when we don't have a family built on God's love? We begin to develop complexities, insecurities, and fall victim to mockers. Then we make fun of others´ flaws and mistakes. And all of this is the result of the lack of identity and having the wrong people anchored in our hearts. We want them to take the place of our real parents because we don´t know God and don´t know that we are the work of His hands. This lack of purpose is what brings confusion into our lives, even producing thoughts and desires of suicide.

If the god we imagine is according to what our parents have been like, we won't be able to achieve the purposes of the Creator. For this reason, it's important to search His Word to find the truth about His unconditional love, character, and personality.

"Behold, children are a heritage from the Lord, the fruit of the womb is a reward" (Psalm 127:3).

You are an inheritance from God to the ones who begot you. Today is a good day to stop fighting! If you haven't talked to your father in many years, give him a call or go visit him and ask for his forgiveness for holding a grudge against him. If he passed away, or you don't know him or don't know where he is, give God that pain you've been carrying.

The deception behind spiritual fatherhood in the words of Jesus Christ is:

"Do not call anyone on earth your father; for One is your Father, He who is in heaven" (Matthew 23:9).

Notice that the first "father" is lowercase. This refers to the biological father. The second time the word is mentioned, it is capitalized, referring to the heavenly Father. This means you only have one spiritual Father: the Creator who is in heaven. God is Spirit, we will go deeper on that later. For now, you need to see that there can only be one "spiritual" Father, although many attribute to themselves the title of "spiritual father". This attribution is not sound doctrine, because in the verse that I just quoted we see Jesus´ instructions. He established that we should not call anyone on earth "father" since we have only one Father, the Most High God. When the heart is completely empty in the fatherhood department, people in that condition look for fathers. Therefore, the Holy Scriptures have been manipulated to establish intermediaries in the relationship that was designed to be between God and men through Jesus Christ, the only mediator between the heavenly Father and His children. How has this misinterpretation and manipulation of the Scriptures come about? We find a few verses about it in the Old Testament:

"And Elisha saw it, and he cried out, ´My father, my father, the chariot of Israel and its horsemen!´ So he saw him no more. And he took hold of his own clothes and tore them into two pieces" (2 Kings 2:12).

Here, the prophet Elisha calls the prophet Elijah his father. This Scripture is widely used among those who establish fatherhood through a mentor or teacher, as the God's Word Translation says it literally:

"When Elisha saw this, he cried out, ´Master! Master! Israel's chariot and horses!´ When he couldn't see Elijah anymore, he grabbed his own garment and tore it in two, to show his grief" (2 Kings 2:12 GW).

It's very important to understand that this verse from the Old Testament does not have the revelation that Jesus Christ came to bring to earth, let's see:

"O righteous Father! The world has not known You, but I have known You; and these have known that You sent Me. And I have declared to them Your name, and will declare it, that the love with which You loved Me may be in them, and I in them" (John 17:25-26).

God gave Jesus Christ an assignment: to reveal Him as the Father. We know that the custom in Israel was to call teachers, mentors, etc. fathers. However, Christ came to establish the reforms of the Father's kingdom. He gave this command when He said, *"Do not call anyone your father..."*, and it's not a suggestion. It's a command that the Son of God established for His people, similar to the teachings He gave about grace:

"You have heard that it was said, 'An eye for an eye and a tooth for a tooth.' But I tell you not to resist an evil person. But whoever slaps you on your right cheek, turn the other to him also" (Matthew 5:38-39).

As we can understand, the standards of grace are much higher than those of the law. It is this same reforming analogy that Christ left to God's people regarding fatherhood, a much higher standard than just the relationship between a prophet and his mentor. Clarifying this, we can say that before the coming of Christ, the fatherhood of God had not been revealed since God's people were separated from Him because of sin.

Christ was the only Son at the time He made this statement since He was the only person on earth who had been directly begotten by the Holy Spirit.

Let's look at this verse:

"Jesus answered, 'If I honor Myself, My honor is nothing. It is My Father who honors Me, of whom you say that He is your God'" (John 8:54).

We can clearly see in the text that the Pharisees, who were experts of the Scriptures, did not know the Father. This is evident through the emphasis Jesus makes, *"... the One you say is your God is My Father..."* (author's paraphrase).

Now, the last Scriptural argument that is used to establish false fatherhood is the words of the apostle Paul when he refers to Timothy as his son:

"I do not write these things to shame you, but as my beloved children I warn you. For though you might have ten thousand instructors in Christ, yet you do not have many fathers; for in

Christ Jesus I have begotten you through the gospel. Therefore I urge you, imitate me. For this reason I have sent Timothy to you, who is my beloved and faithful son in the Lord, who will remind you of my ways in Christ, as I teach everywhere in every church" (1 Corinthians 4:14-17).

In this passage, the apostle Paul is speaking to the Corinthian church, which he had raised through his work as an apostle of Jesus Christ. This verse has been used to establish a fatherhood through the servants of God. But notice that he begins by saying that he is writing to those who are *"as his beloved children."* This speaks of the close relationship the apostle had with that church, and he uses an analogy about fatherhood and the begetting of a child. However, the one who begets "heavenly fatherhood" is the Spirit of God through the spirit of adoption. There are only two ways of being begotten, through the flesh (biological father) and through the Spirit, as we see in the following Scripture:

"For you did not receive the spirit of bondage again to fear, but you received the Spirit of adoption by whom we cry out, ´Abba, Father.´ The Spirit Himself bears witness with our spirit that we are children of God" (Romans 8:15-16).

Could it be that the apostle Paul was unaware of the Scriptures when he called himself the spiritual father of the Corinthian church? Could it be that he had not listened to the words of Jesus that forbid calling any man on earth "father"? I don't think so! We know that the Holy Scripture doesn't contradict itself. Therefore, we can conclude that the apostle was using an analogy with the fatherhood of God. After all, he was the one who wrote the book to the Romans, which clearly establishes that spiritual fatherhood is directed by the Spirit of God and through Jesus Christ. Let's see:

"But as many as received Him, to them He gave the right to become children of God, to those who believe in His name: who were born, not of blood, nor of the will of the flesh, nor of the will of man, but of God" (John 1:12-13).

In this passage, we see even more clearly that the adoption of spiritual children of the Father cannot take place by human will. The Scriptures also point out that it cannot happen through flesh and blood either, and that includes the apostle Paul of course.

This great apostle not only speaks about his fatherhood to the Corinthians but also mentions a special relationship with his most beloved disciple, Timothy. Let's take a look:

"To Timothy, a true son in the faith: Grace, mercy, and peace from God our Father and Jesus Christ our Lord" (1 Timothy 1:2).

This is the way Paul addressed Timothy, he calls him *"a true son in the faith"*. This does not mean that Timothy was Paul's son, but that the apostle had taught him, instructed him and that this servant of God was like a father to Timothy. He gave him affirmation, assurance, and had a very close relationship with this young pastor who had earned Paul's trust and love because of his authentic faith in the gospel. However, in this same passage, when Paul blesses Timothy he mentions *"God our Father."* It is also important to note that Paul had no children, so Timothy was like a son to him. Let›s see what he wrote to him in the following passage:

"I thank God, whom I serve with a pure conscience, as my forefathers did, as without ceasing I remember you in my prayers night and day, greatly desiring to see you, being mindful of your tears, that I may be filled with joy, when I call to remembrance the genuine faith that is in you, which dwelt first in your grandmother Lois and your mother Eunice, and I am persuaded is in you also. Therefore I remind you to stir up the gift of God which is in you through the laying on of my hands. For God has not given us a spirit of fear, but of power and of love and of a sound mind" (2 Timothy 1:3-7).

The apostle´s moving words show us that Timothy wasn´t just a disciple; there was a relationship between them that involved the soul. Paul knew Timothy´s family and was familiar with his mother and grandmother´s faith. He also gave him advice about the gift he received when the apostle prayed for him and ministered to him by the laying on of hands, which shows their close-knit relationship. Finally, he reminds him that he has been empowered with courage and not fear. However, we see Timothy is a member of a family where the male figure was absent. Where was his grandfather? Where was his father? These are questions I ask about his life, just like I ask them about many people I meet. Now, I understand that Timothy was like a reward for Paul on earth, a blessing amidst obvious dishonors and sufferings that Paul had endured as an apostle of Christ. Let's analyze an important fact about Timothy in the following Scripture:

"Then he came to Derbe and Lystra. And behold, a certain disciple was there, named Timothy, the son of a certain Jewish woman who believed, but his father was Greek" (Acts 16:1).

In this passage, we find a mystery. Scripture tells us that Timothy´s mom was Jewish and a believer, and includes a "but" (which means opposition). Timothy's father was Greek, and logically I deduce that he wasn't a believer. I really think that there's a deception about fatherhood in the Church that is also present in every sphere of religion and society; from the popes of the Vatican, the Catholic priests, to the Christian pastors, the apostles, to the freemasons, to the satanists and santeros. Everyone wants to be a father. The deception is in the form of a pyramid, hierarchy, or Nicolaism in which the devil has distorted the fatherhood of God, establishing intermediaries. They become bridges between God and men, invalidating the work of the cross of Calvary. The work of Jesus on the cross is the only thing that removed separation and constituted Christ as High Priest and mediator between the heavenly Father and His children. In many congregations, I´ve seen the pastor or apostle become the father of the church members. Now, suppose that among these members there are orphans or children of divorced parents, single mothers, or from adulterous relationships. These people cling to this "spiritual father", but he commits adultery or divorces his wife and leaves the congregation.

Or what about the young man who never met his biological father and the pastor tells him that he will be his father, but then this member commits a sin and is expelled from the congregation. My last example to make my point is what happens when the pastor who said he would be their father dies? How do you think the "adopted" members of the church feel?

The feeling of orphanhood will simply be reawakened and the wound will be even deeper. This kind of fatherhood creates an expectation in their hearts of what they were looking for. But if the man of God fails, the "adoptee" will never believe in anything that has to do with fatherhood again, because this leader failed due to his human condition.

To constitute a spiritual fatherhood upon the pastor is a very heavy burden that no servant of God can bear because their "adopted" children will demand perfection and faithfulness. The only One who can uphold a spiritual child is the heavenly Father. Once He begets a child through the spirit of adoption, He will never leave them or take away their legal rights as a child of God. Throughout the Scriptures, we see who Christ ordained for His work on earth:

"And He Himself gave some to be apostles, some prophets, some evangelists, and some pastors and teachers, for the equipping of the saints for the work of ministry, for the edifying of the body of Christ" (Ephesians 4:11-12).

In these five ministries is the fullness of the Lord Jesus Christ. He is the Apostle of apostles, Prophet of prophets,

Evangelist of evangelists, Pastor of pastors, and Teacher of teachers. Fatherhood was never allotted when the vocations were given by His authority. On the contrary, He always made it clear that He represented His Father on earth. Christ is an example in everything.

"For I have given you an example, that you should do as I have done to you. Most assuredly, I say to you, a servant is not greater than his master; nor is he who is sent greater than he who sent him" (John 13:15-16).

In each of these callings, we see the Lord´s example because Christ is everything in the five ministries. Being an apostle, a pastor, or exercising any of these ministries does not make you a father. Caring for a person, guiding them to the truth, and teaching them the gospel makes you a pastor. Some apostles say that only they can reveal fatherhood because of what Paul had with Timothy. With arguments like this, they impose hierarchies that Christ did not establish. If the apostle had the power to reveal fatherhood then what did Christ come to do? Timothy was like an orphan son for Paul and so is the Church seeking fatherhood in men. It is true that Paul loved him, taught him, and ministered to him. This would be the ideal relationship between a man of God who has been anointed to serve in the church, and every person wounded in the fatherhood department. However, we must analyse that an apostle or pastor cannot have a close relationship with all its members from a pulpit, nor a priest with a mass on Sundays, and not to mention the mega-churches that are established through networks. It's impossible for the disciple who attends one of these congregations to receive what Timothy received from the apostle Paul —a personal relationship, closeness to family, and letters addressed to him— from a pulpit. We all know the value and the great privilege God gives us in having a mentor, but we also understand that it is not possible to have a close relationship with everyone. Elisha had Elijah and Timothy had Paul, but this is not the case for all of God's people. What we can all have is communion with the Holy Spirit who reveals our true Father to us. Mentors have a God-assigned disciple to train so then they share the teachings with others. Although it´s true that the disciple can minister what they've received, the7 still need a close-knit relationship where there is familiarity and trust. We understand that despite all the love Paul had for Timothy, and his desire for him to overcome cowardice, which is typical in orphanhood, Timothy had to receive the Holy Spirit, not by the will of Paul, but of God. How many members in churches live without the spirit of adoption? There are pastors and priests who demand honor as fathers from the pulpit, but who honors the heavenly Father?

This is why the Lord says:

"Render therefore to all their due: taxes to whom taxes are due, customs to whom customs, fear to whom fear, honor to whom honor" (Romans 13:7).

This precept is not only for God's ministers but for every human being. This means that whoever is in a position of honor should be honored. But it is one thing to honor someone as a pastor, teacher, apostle, evangelist, or prophet, and another thing to honor them as "fathers" when Jesus Christ made it clear that this should not be done. Yet it is necessary to clarify it again because the same thing is happening today as in Jesus´ time. Many have established themselves as fathers, contrary to the biblical precept:

"´A son honors his father, and a servant his master. If then I am the Father, where is My honor? And if I am a Master, where is My reverence?´ Says the Lord of hosts to you priests who despise My name. Yet you say, 'In what way have we despised Your name?´" (Malachi 1:6).

This quote from the prophet Malachi shows God's anger at being dishonored as a Father. Really this honor that He speaks of is the kind of honor that a son gives his father.

The Lord is a God of order, therefore He established the authority to manifest His kingdom, which is structured under hierarchical authority. However, Satan has always sought to disorganize and copy all of God's designs by imitating and plagiarizing them. We´ve already seen that every human being was separated from God and therefore became helpless, but God's desire has always been to restore order in creation. The last Old Testament prophecy, before Christ came to earth as a man, reveals God's desire to prepare the way for heavenly fatherhood:

"Behold, I will send you Elijah the prophet before the coming of the great and dreadful day of the Lord. And he will turn

the hearts of the fathers to the children, and the hearts of the children to their fathers, lest I come and strike the earth with a curse" (Malachi 4:5-6).

This is God's last declaration to His people, so we deduce that this passage is extremely important. Why would these be God's closing words in the Old Testament? It took 400 years for them to hear His voice again. In this passage, the Lord is speaking of earthly fatherhood. This needed to be restored before He could reestablish the heavenly one, which is why Satan has seized the order of fatherhood.

Up until this point, I´ve addressed the children because they must forgive their parents and honor them. I reiterate the order of the Lord: "*...He will turn the hearts of fathers towards their children...*" Many parents know this verse by heart, they know that their children should honor them, but how many of them are willing to restore the relationship with their children? How many can acknowledge that they´ve been hurt and ask them to forgive them? In many cases, when the father has the spirit of orphanhood and is a servant of God, his children develop problems relating to the Creator. God is Father and He did not sit idly waiting for His children to come to Him. Instead, He sent Jesus Christ to mend the separation. The passage above also mentions the wound of a curse that comes because of unrestored fatherhood.

God is **Father** and He sent **Jesus Christ** to mend the separation

What does God mean by the phrase *"I will turn"*? In the Hebrew language, the same word has many meanings. Some of them include: to appease, repent, reestablish, restore, make restitution.

So the last intervention of Almighty God in the Old Testament was the promise that the spirit of Elijah would come with this assignment, let's see if it was fulfilled:

"And he will turn many of the children of Israel to the Lord their God. He will also go before Him in the spirit and power of Elijah, 'to turn the hearts of the fathers to the children,' and the disobedient to the wisdom of the just, to make ready a people prepared for the Lord" (Luke 1:16-17).

This is part of the prophecy that the angel Gabriel gave to the priest Zacharias, John the Baptist's father. He told him he would have a son named John and said the words above when explaining John´s assignment. The precision of the Holy Scriptures is impressive since the preaching of John the prophet was characterized by his calling to repentance. In this passage, we also see the condition of the hearts of those to whom John was sent, *"...and the disobedient to the wisdom of the just."* Rebellion is one of the most distinctive characteristics in orphans, since to the extent that children rebel against parents they rebel against God. Although John declared this to the people, they didn't understand that the promise God had given in Malachi was being fulfilled before their very eyes. Now, what was God's plan? That the fathers would forgive their children and the children forgive their fathers. Therefore, the relationship could be restored and the way be prepared to receive the heavenly fatherhood that Jesus Christ would reveal. For this reason, John said that he would prepare the way for the One to come. When Christ was baptized by John in the Jordan, God made the first declaration that Jesus is His Son. At this moment, righteousness was fulfilled and the fatherhood of God began to be revealed through Christ.

John the Baptist was the instrument God used to call people to repentance. Once this was accomplished, the hearts of those who obeyed would be prepared to receive the Spirit of adoption and they would be restored through heavenly fatherhood. Let's see the words of Jesus in this regard:

"And His disciples asked Him, saying, 'Why then do the scribes say that Elijah must come first?' Jesus answered and said to them, 'Indeed, Elijah is coming first and will restore all things. But I say to you that Elijah has come already, and they did not know him but did to him whatever they wished. Likewise the Son of Man is also about to suffer at their hands.' Then the disciples understood that He spoke to them of John the Baptist" (Matthew 17:10-13).

The scribes were very familiar with the prophecy given through Malachi and were waiting for Elijah. However, they did not recognize him because of the hardness of their hearts. Now, what was the restoration *"of all things"* that they expected? The restoration of earthly fatherhood, the revelation of God's fatherhood, and the relationship man had lost with Him because of sin. But they did not receive it, they beheaded John and the majority rejected his message. He suffered because of the assignment God had entrusted him. There are some religious people who are only attentive to power and the hierarchy of authority, just like what the people did to Jesus. John was right when he said:

"´Repent, for the kingdom of heaven is at hand!´ For this is he who was spoken of by the prophet Isaiah, saying: ´The voice of one crying in the wilderness: 'Prepare the way of the Lord; make His paths straight´´" (Matthew 3:2-3).

This was the reason for John's message, but repentance for what? His big assignment was to restore earthly fatherhood as the preparation of the way for Jesus to reveal heavenly fatherhood. This same message from John characterized the beginning of Jesus' ministry on two different levels: one earthly and the other spiritual.

"From that time Jesus began to preach and to say, ´Repent, for the kingdom of heaven is at hand.´" (Matthew 4:17)

There can be no kingdom without God and there is no God without repentance. This blessing comes through the restoration of earthly fatherhood that prepares the way to receive heavenly fatherhood and the restoration of all things. A person in orphanhood does not have an identity. They can't possess the inheritance that belongs to them as a child of God, nor are they able to govern the earth, subdue it and rule it according to His will. This is the restoration of all things; man returning, not only to the condition of being a child of God, but also an heir. There is no contradiction between John´s preaching and Jesus´

preaching since the prophet only cried out for the voice of Jesus to be heard. We've established that first, the image of the earthly father had to be given, then the image of the heavenly Father would come. In the same way, there was harmony between John the Baptist and Jesus Christ. First, one operated on the earthly and physical realm and the other on the spiritual and heavenly realm. It is necessary that all righteousness be fulfilled according to the design and order that God has established.

"John answered, saying to all, ´I indeed baptize you with water; but One mightier than I is coming, whose sandal strap I am not worthy to loose. He will baptize you with the Holy Spirit and fire´" (Luke 3:16).

According to this verse, baptism in water is first and then the baptism of the Holy Spirit and fire. On the other hand, we find Satan´s great scheme manipulating the fatherhood of God. This deception is similar to idolatry because it doesn't matter who you worship, if it's not the One true God it's idolatry. The enemy does the same with fatherhood when you acknowledge anyone who is not your earthly father and heavenly Father as your father.

Now, let's look at the personality traits of an orphan and what feelings they harbor:

"Because I delivered the poor who cried out, the fatherless and the one who had no helper" (Job 29:12).

This passage shows us that orphans typically live with a lack of help. An orphan feels that no one is for them, that they fight alone, and that they don't have any help. If their earthly father left them or was never present, these feelings begin to take over their personality. They begin to think, *"I am my burden. I carry life on my own back."*

But, the Scriptures state:

"Hear, O Lord, and have mercy on me; Lord, be my helper!" (Psalm 30:10).

Knowing the Father as our helper is a conviction that is revealed to our lives.

"Happy is he who has the God of Jacob for his help, whose hope is in the Lord his God" (Psalm 146:5).

Yes, there is a helper: God, the heavenly Father. For this reason, the orphan who feels helpless is embraced by Him:

"But You have seen, for You observe trouble and grief, to repay it by Your hand. The helpless commits himself to You; You are the helper of the fatherless" (Psalm 10:14).

A mark in the orphan's soul is feeling like they're the object of humiliation, ridicule, and abuse. They feel no one is protecting them, they feel completely helpless and tired. They work but live without food, shelter, and the necessary things needed to survive. However, the previous passage shows that the Father protects all those who feel this way.

"Some snatch the fatherless from the breast,and take a pledge from the poor" (Job 24:9).

"To do justice to the fatherless and the oppressed, that the man of the earth may oppress no more" (Psalm 10:18).

"Defend the poor and fatherless; do justice to the afflicted and needy" (Psalm 82:3),

In these verses, we see a few of the characteristics found in someone's soul who has been wounded by orphanhood: deprived, unprotected, afflicted, weak, oppressed, and forsaken. Faced with all these difficulties, they develop a fearful, distrustful, and aggressive personality. They feel they need to protect themselves, they don't easily allow strangers into their lives, and they tend to be very reserved and superficial.

"For as he thinks in his heart, so is he" (Proverbs 23:7a).

We know that Jesus Christ is our Master in everything. So let's analyze His identity and the belief system He had about Himself in order to compare it with ours.

The Son´s personality:

"Then the angel said to her, ´Do not be afraid, Mary, for you have found favor with God. And behold, you will conceive in your womb and bring forth a Son, and shall call His name Jesus. He will be great, and will be called the Son of the Highest; and the Lord God will give Him the throne of His father David.

And He will reign over the house of Jacob forever, and of His kingdom there will be no end.´ Then Mary said to the angel, ´How can this be, since I do not know a man?´ And the angel answered and said to her, ´The Holy Spirit will come upon you, and the power of the Highest will overshadow you; therefore, also, that Holy One who is to be born will be called the Son of God´" (Luke 1:30-35).

In this passage, we can see that Jesus Christ was begotten by the Holy Spirit. This is the first characteristic of the Lord Jesus. He was not begotten by His earthly father, Joseph, who in this case was His stepfather. The Most High God chose Joseph to sustain Him and His mother, but Jesus´ identity did not come from him. Joseph was only an instrument chosen by God, just like Mary.

This is the great difference between those of us who were created and adopted by the Father through Jesus Christ. We see the unique personality of One who was begotten by the Holy Spirit, although He also had a stepfather on earth.

When Jesus was 12, He got lost in the crowd and was out of His parents´ sight. But the response He gave to Mary's claim when they found Him was:

"So when they saw Him, they were amazed; and His mother said to Him, ´Son, why have You done this to us? Look, Your father and I have sought You anxiously.´ And He said to them, ´Why did you seek Me? Did you not know that I must be about My Father's business?´" (Luke 2: 48-49).

What business was Jesus talking about? Was He referring to Joseph´s carpentry business? No, He was talking about His heavenly Father. Scripture says that when they found Him He was hearing the law and asking about it in the temple; how did Jesus know about such business at a young age?

"All things have been delivered to Me by My Father, and no one knows who the Son is except the Father, and who the Father is except the Son, and the one to whom the Son wills to reveal Him" (Luke 10:22).

How were all these things given to Jesus? How did Jesus meet the Father? How does Jesus reveal the Father? In this Scripture, we clearly see that the only way to know the heavenly Father is by allowing Christ to reveal Him. We can prepare our hearts by restoring our earthly fatherhood and crying out for the heavenly fatherhood that is only given by the will of Christ. You can only know the Father by having the Spirit of the Son. However, it is evident that all things were given to Christ because He was begotten by the Holy Spirit. Let's look at a fragment of Jesus' dialogue with the Samaritan woman:

"The woman said to Him, ´I know that Messiah is coming´ (who is called Christ). ´When He comes, He will tell us all things.´ Jesus said to her, ´I who speak to you am He´"
(John 4: 25-26).

Notice how He spoke of Himself, *"I am."* Who told Jesus that He was the Messiah, the Christ? Do you know who you are?

"Pilate therefore said to Him, 'Are You a king then?' Jesus answered, 'You say rightly that I am a king. For this cause I was born, and for this cause I have come into the world, that I should bear witness to the truth. Everyone who is of the truth hears My voice'" (John 18:37).

How did Jesus know the reason for which He was born and why He came into the world? This is the result of God's fatherhood; discovering the purpose for which you were born.

"Jesus said to them, 'My food is to do the will of Him who sent Me, and to finish His work.'" (John 4:34)

The Son's authority:

"Then Jesus answered and said to them, 'Most assuredly, I say to you, the Son can do nothing of Himself, but what He sees the Father do; for whatever He does, the Son also does in like manner. For the Father loves the Son, and shows Him all things that He Himself does; and He will show Him greater works than these, that you may marvel. For as the Father raises the dead and gives life to them, even so the Son gives life to whom He will. For the Father judges no one, but has committed all judgment to the Son, that all should honor the Son just as they honor the Father. He who does not honor the Son does not honor the Father who sent Him'" (John 5: 19-23).

Here, we see an authority subdued to the will of the Father. Christ didn't want to do anything outside of the assignment the Father had given Him or do anything by

Himself. He said that whatever He did, He had first seen His Father do. This is the same even in the earthly realm; children do what they see their parents do, good or bad. They are an extension of their parents, this is the strength that comes with fatherhood.

Witnesses of Christ:

"I can of Myself do nothing. As I hear, I judge; and My judgment is righteous, because I do not seek My own will but the will of the Father who sent Me" (John 5:30).

Jesus shows us what absolute obedience to His Father looks like.

"But I have a greater witness than John's; for the works which the Father has given Me to finish—the very works that I do—bear witness of Me, that the Father has sent Me. And the Father Himself, who sent Me, has testified of Me" (John 5:36-37a).

Everyone who suffers from orphanhood is concerned about what others think about them. They have a very large reflection of rejection, but Jesus's words show that He wasn't interested in what people said about Him. His Father was the One who bore witness about Him and, not just the Father, but the works Jesus did by the power He received from the Father.

Jesus, the bread of life:

"And Jesus said to them, ´I am the bread of life. He who comes to Me shall never hunger, and he who believes in Me shall never thirst´" (John 6:35).

These are the convictions that Jesus had about Himself. Although He was the most humble of all the men who have walked the earth, He did not have false humility. He knew who He was.

"All that the Father gives Me will come to Me, and the one who comes to Me I will by no means cast out. For I have come down from heaven, not to do My own will, but the will of Him who sent Me" (John 6:37-38).

In this passage, we see that Jesus did not have to fight for His inheritance. He understood that He would receive everything because His Father had given it to Him. He knew His place before coming to earth; and again, this statement is characterized by His obedience and submission.

Now let's see how others reacted to these truths Jesus gave:

"The Jews then complained about Him, because He said, ´I am the bread which came down from heaven.´ And they said, ´Is not this Jesus, the son of Joseph, whose father and mother we know?´" (John 6:41-42a).

Like these Jews, many people can murmur about your identity, but you´re not what people think or say about you. You are what God says about you.

"As the living Father sent Me, and I live because of the Father, so he who feeds on Me will live because of Me." (John 6:57)

The Father was Jesus´ source of life that set Him apart.

Jesus´ timing:

"Then Jesus said to them, ´My time has not yet come, but your time is always ready´" (John 7:6).

When you live under heavenly fatherhood, you understand that your seasons are in His hands. No one can do anything against you if not allowed by the strict sovereignty of God.

Jesus´ doctrine:

"Jesus answered them and said, ´My doctrine is not Mine, but His who sent Me´" (John 7:16).

This means that He did not come with His own teachings, but with those that the Father had given Him.

Jesus the Christ:

"Then Jesus cried out, as He taught in the temple, saying, ´You both know Me, and you know where I am from; and I have not come of Myself, but He who sent Me is true, whom you do not know. But I know Him, for I am from Him, and He sent Me´" (John 7:28-29).

Christ knew where He came from; from the Father, not from Joseph. This is the same conviction that those of us who are children of God have in our hearts.

"Then Jesus said to them, 'I shall be with you a little while longer, and then I go to Him who sent Me'" (John 7:33).

Jesus knew where He came from and where He was going.

He is the light of the world:

"Then Jesus spoke to them again, saying, 'I am the light of the world. He who follows Me shall not walk in darkness, but have the light of life'" (John 8:12).

Where is Jesus from? Let's read His own answer.

"And He said to them, 'You are from beneath; I am from above. You are of this world; I am not of this world'" (John 8:23).

"Then Jesus said to them, 'When you lift up the Son of Man, then you will know that I am He, and that I do nothing of Myself; but as My Father taught Me, I speak these things'" (John 8:28).

The Father taught Jesus directly, through His Holy Spirit.

"And He who sent Me is with Me. The Father has not left Me alone, for I always do those things that please Him" (John 8:29).

Jesus Christ was convinced that the Father was with Him. He didn't feel lonely, which is another one of the characteristics that drive the orphan´s personality. Although Jesus didn't have a wife or children, and the disciples whom He had asked to pray with Him fell asleep, He knew He was not alone.

The truth will make us free:

"I speak what I have seen with My Father, and you do what you have seen with your father" (John 8:38).

In this passage, we see that many heard what their parents told them about the Father. They inherited patterns and traditions, but Christ had seen Him. This is why Job, after walking through a very intense trial and coming to really know God, made the following statement:

"I have heard of You by the hearing of the ear,but now my eye sees You" (Job 42:5).

Many claim to love God but hate the Son, such as the Muslims, Jehovah's Witnesses, among many other religions, all based on error.

"Jesus said to them, ´If God were your Father, you would love Me, for I proceeded forth and came from God; nor have I come of Myself, but He sent Me´" (John 8:42).

"Jesus answered, ´If I honor Myself, My honor is nothing. It is My Father who honors Me, of whom you say that He is your God´" (John 8:54).

The glory Christ had, He received from the heavenly Father. Orphans seek to be recognized, that is, they seek the glory of men. But really, they are not seeking glory, they are seeking boastfulness.

Jesus´ unity with the Father and His works:

"I and My Father are one" (John 10:30).

This verse points to the source of the Lord Jesus Christ´s power: unity with His Father. In this unit there were no contradictions, personal interests or division; they were united in the same purpose because One´s achievements were the achievements of the Others as well. This was possible because Jesus emptied Himself, He had no desire outside of His Father's will; His will and His Father's were the same.

"Do you say of Him whom the Father sanctified and sent into the world, 'You are blaspheming,' because I said, 'I am the Son of God'? If I do not do the works of My Father, do not believe Me; but if I do, though you do not believe Me, believe the works, that you may know and believe that the Father is in Me, and I in Him" (John 10: 36-38).

Jesus was convinced that He was the Son of God and therefore did His works.

Jesus´ trust:

"Then they took away the stone from the place where the dead man was lying. And Jesus lifted up His eyes and said, ´Father, I thank You that You have heard Me. And I know that You always hear Me, but because of the people who are standing by I said this, that they may believe that You sent Me´" (John 11:41-42).

Jesus knew that every time He prayed to His Father, His Father listened. As we read earlier in Psalms, the orphan believes that they are forsaken and that God doesn't hear their cry. When they pray, they do so with doubt and unbelief, asking themself if God exists.

Jesus´ obedience:

"Now My soul is troubled, and what shall I say? 'Father, save Me from this hour'? But for this purpose I came to this hour" (John 12:27).

Although Jesus was afflicted by the suffering involved in the purpose of the cross, His obedience overrode His affliction. The Son´s submission was not governed by the soul, but by the Spirit. He knew He needed to fulfill the prophetic destination of His life which was to die on the cross and fulfill His assignment on earth.

"For I have not spoken on My own authority; but the Father who sent Me gave Me a command, what I should say and what I should speak" (John 12:49).

Every one of His statements came from His Father's mouth; they were not His own convictions or idle words. Jesus knew Who did the works and was under His authority.

"Do you not believe that I am in the Father, and the Father in Me? The words that I speak to you I do not speak on My own authority; but the Father who dwells in Me does the works" (John 14:10).

"You have heard Me say to you, 'I am going away and coming back to you.' If you loved Me, you would rejoice because I said, 'I am going to the Father,' for My Father is greater than I" (John 14:28).

Because Jesus knew that the Father was greater than Him, He was always meek and humbly submitted to this truth. He did not have low self-esteem.

Jesus knew that He was loved:

"As the Father loved Me, I also have loved you; abide in Me" (John 15:9).

This conviction kept Jesus from being afraid, despite the harassment He suffered from the religious people of His time. The love of His Father was His protection, a shield, and His reality. He was loved and loved everyone according to the measure of love He had received.

Jesus knew that He was the heir to everything:

"All things that the Father has are Mine. Therefore I said that He will take of Mine and declare it to you" (John 16:15).

Orphans believe they have nothing, just like the older brother in the Parable of the Prodigal Son, whom we will analyze in the chapter about grace. That is why someone with this feeling of orphanhood is able to sell their soul in an attempt to fill that void but end up full of bitterness. This is why Jesus did not treasure anything, He knew that everything His Father had was His. Jesus knew that He was His Father´s heir.

Jesus knew He wasn't alone and declares it again:

"Indeed the hour is coming, yes, has now come, that you will be scattered, each to his own, and will leave Me alone. And yet I am not alone, because the Father is with Me" (John 16:32).

Jesus´ trust

"Or do you think that I cannot now pray to My Father, and He will provide Me with more than twelve legions of angels?" (Matthew 26:53).

This was the conviction Jesus had amidst attacks of fear. He knew that if He cried out, His Father would do everything necessary to free Him from any situation. Even so, He understood that no one could do more to Him than what was in God's established plan. The army of heaven is submitted to the voice of the Father and to the service of His children.

Jesus´ reverent fear and His submitted will to the Father

"He went a little farther and fell on His face, and prayed, saying, ´O My Father, if it is possible, let this cup pass from Me; nevertheless, not as I will, but as You will´" (Matthew 26:39).

"Again, a second time, He went away and prayed, saying, ´O My Father, if this cup cannot pass away from Me unless I drink it, Your will be done´" (Matthew 26:42).

All these verses show us what Jesus believed in His heart about Himself and His Father.

Many people think that Jesus believed this because He was the Son of God, and it is so, but this same belief system is available to anyone who receives the spirit of adoption. As we have seen, the opposite of Jesus´ beliefs are those that are harbored in the feeling of orphanhood: fear, loneliness, poverty, intimidation, absurdity, religiosity, condemnation, rejection, and a false identity.

Like I´ve said before, forsakenness is the condition of man when separated from the Father. Therefore, I dare to say that during the crucifixion, Jesus Christ also experienced orphanhood.

"And about the ninth hour Jesus cried out with a loud voice, saying, 'Eli, Eli, lama sabachthani?' that is, 'My God, My God, why have You forsaken Me?'" (Matthew 27:46).

What happened to Jesus´ faith and belief system? Weren't these the same words in Psalm 22:1 written during the psalmist´s distress? You can see that Jesus' nature was as human as ours. He truly felt the anguish of the separation between Him and the Father. The suffering was so great that Jesus felt God was not His Father, which is why He calls Him *"My God."* The forsakenness that Jesus suffered at that moment in His life was the agony of the cross of Calvary, as He carried all of our sins on His body to reconcile us with the Father. This pain is similar to that felt by the person experiencing orphanhood, Jesus had never been far from His Father since when He was begotten by the Holy Spirit. This was the only time that Christ felt He was without His Father during His life on earth.

Christ told the disciples that He would not leave them as orphans. Although John 14:15-18 speaks of the coming of the Holy Spirit, verse 18 reaffirms the fatherhood of the Father. This is why Jesus used this kind of language with them, even though He had never experienced orphanhood.

"I will not leave you orphans; I will come to you" (John 14:18).

Was this a physical orphanhood that Jesus talked to the disciples about? Was He referring to people who did not have biological parents? The answer is no. Orphanhood is in every human being as long as they lack the presence of the heavenly Father in their lives. If Jesus used this wording, it's because they were orphans.

What does *orphan* mean in the original Greek? The word Jesus uses here is *orfanó*; uncertain and afflicted. This is the description for those without parents. This definition teaches us that an orphan is uncertain and afflicted. We know that the New Testament was written in Greek and translated into different languages, but the Old Testament was written in Hebrew. Let's see what orphan means in the original Hebrew, according to the story about an orphan named Esther:

"And Mordecai had brought up Hadassah, that is, Esther, his uncle's daughter, for she had neither father nor mother. The young woman was lovely and beautiful. When her father and mother died, Mordecai took her as his own daughter" (Esther 2:7).

Esther was her cousin's adopted daughter because her father and mother had died. We already know that this Hebrew girl´s identity did not come from her cousin and that the promise for those who lose their parents is that God Himself cares for them. But how many children are like her? Raised by an uncle or grandparents? In the original, this Hebrew word means: *Ayin*; from the primitive root, which means to be nothing or not to exist, non-entity (of no value). The word is used as a negative description meaning to lack, to be a thing, to disappear, to not have, not have enough, orphan, incurable, inscrutable, infinite, die, nothing, nobody, none, number, perish (Spanish Strong Concordance: 369, compare with 370).

The meaning of this word is very strong. In the definition, we find a great discovery about orphanhood; when we are in this condition *we are like nothing, nobody has an identity, and we don't exist*, which is why it causes such a deep wound. Look at how the definition itself says "incurable", "infinite". This reference leads me to the definition of another Hebrew word: *Ayin*; probable. Identical with 369 in the sense of a question (compare with 336) *Where?* (only in connection with the preposition. Prefix: From where?) *Where, from where?* Where do I come from? What was I born for? Where am I going? Here is the answer to these questions that have always been on people's minds: *without Divine fatherhood, there is no purpose; I don't know where I come from or where I'm going.*

The only One who can give completely clear answers to these uncertainties is the heavenly Father. Not understanding this reality is what causes the lack of purpose that exists in many people's lives.

For this reason, Christ says that He will not leave us to be orphans. He promises to send the Father's promise, the Holy Spirit, so that separation with the heavenly Father may be removed, thus eliminating forsakenness. Heavenly fatherhood gives meaning to our existence and reveals God's plan for each life. It is for this reason that no one can take the position of a spiritual father; only the heavenly Father can give you the identity that was given to Jesus Christ.

Let's look at the Father's promises

"God sets the solitary in families; He brings out those who are bound into prosperity; but the rebellious dwell in a dry land" (Psalm 68:6).

God makes you dwell in family. If you don't have a family, if you were abandoned by your father, if you feel forsaken even with earthly parents, God brings you out of that affliction to the prosperity that comes with His protection. Note that rebellion is mentioned in this promise, as well as in the angel's words to Zacharias when he spoke of John the Baptist´s assignment, *"He will turn the hearts of the fathers to the children, and the disobedient to the wisdom."* As long as you are in rebellion against your parents, you cannot live as a family, on the contrary, *"you will live on dry land."* If you feel like "no one›s child", forgive and take hold of what the heavenly Father did to rescue you!

"But as many as received Him, to them He gave the right to become children of God, to those who believe in His name" (John 1:12).

Every human being is a child of God, His creation. But we become children of God when we receive Jesus Christ and believe in His name. Only to those of us who believe in Jesus, God gives us the right to be His children; we are not just servants who have accepted Christ as Savior and Lord, we are also sons and daughters. We are not the Lord´s slaves, but children of the Most High God. What happens in our lives when we are children?

"Therefore you are no longer a slave but a son, and if a son, then an heir of God through Christ" (Galatians 4:7).

We have what Jesus Christ possesses. All that the Father has is ours; we are heirs. This is the restoration in our lives of all that was lost in Eden. Finally, the identity of a child of God:

"For I say, through the grace given to me, to everyone who is among you, not to think of himself more highly than he ought to think, but to think soberly, as God has dealt to each one a measure of faith" (Romans 12:3).

Orphanhood distorts the identity of mankind, exalting them to pride or humiliating them to contempt. On the other hand, identity is developed by faith in the Holy Scriptures. The precise measure of identity is having a correct self-concept like Jesus did of Himself. You are who the Father says you are.

Prayer to receive God's Fatherhood and Identity

(Orphanhood)

Creator of all things, today I come before You because I believe that You are God, and I want to know You as my Father.

I ask You to forgive me for the pain that I harbored in my heart, for not coming to You for You to heal my wounds and show me the way, who is Jesus, Your beloved Son. I ask You for forgiveness because I gave more importance to my emotions than to You, which prevented me from finding Your comfort, the revelation of Your truth, and Your power to heal me. Today, I recognize that I need You; I surrender before You. I confess that I am full of insecurities, that I feel far from You, without help, forsaken, and alone.

Jesus, with a humble and sincere heart, I ask You to show me the heavenly Father, to reveal the Father to me and thus heal my soul, my life, my heart, and my whole being. Today I give up following my own paths, I give up following the design of this world because I desire to have Your design in my life. Today I decide to forgive as I have been forgiven by You and reconcile with my earthly father. I know it will not be easy, but as You hold me by Your right hand, I will do it and will achieve it because this is Your will for my life. I renounce rebellion, independence, the orphan spirit, and the curse of the orphan and bastard because You have redeemed me from the curse.

I want Your revelation as my Father because I long to leave the pain, bitterness, sadness, loneliness, insecurity, and fear behind. I no longer want to feel helpless and forsaken. I want to receive from You the Spirit of God that cries out, "ABBA FATHER!" Father, send Your Spirit of adoption into my life, I beg You. Teach me what it means to be a son/daughter because I have never known a father.

God and Heavenly Father, I thank You for Your great love. You wanted to find me and embrace me, so You sent Jesus Christ to die for me. Thank You because You reconciled me to You before I met You. You never wanted to be far from me nor for me to be far from You, but sin separated us. Thank You because Your love found me; because from now on I am no longer an orphan, I know that You are my Father and I find my worth in You. I was not an accident, You formed me with a loving and divine purpose. Thank You Father for Your Son Jesus Christ and for the Comforter. Thank You Jesus Christ for Your obedience until death in order to reveal the Father to us. Help me to be more like You. Father, I ask all of this in Jesus´ name. Amen.

Chapter 2

Fatherhood and Love

(Fear)

Fear is an evil force that makes man feel miserable. But, where does fear come from? It comes from the absence of love. It makes a person feel like they are being punished. It is able to establish unreal events in a person's imagination, though they perceive them as if they were real. Fear is extremely dangerous in the life of any human being. It uses a person's imagination to bring into the real world the scenarios the person has visualized in their mind. Let's see how this works: faith allows you to see the circumstances spiritually and has a creative power subject to God's sovereignty. For example, a child may say, "When I grow up I want to be a doctor." They have activated their capacity to imagine and has linked it to the prior knowledge that doctors exist. If they add faith, they could see themself dressed as a doctor and play like one.

Imagining it and believing it will make it easier for you to achieve it. That's faith, it´s creative.

Similar to faith, fear has the capacity to trust, but in a negative way. This is completely opposite to faith in Jesus Christ. Fear´s objective is to produce punishment and then for those fears to come true. Imagination is made up of the images that are produced in the mind of the human being.

Let's take a look at what God's Word says about fear:

"For the thing I greatly feared has come upon me, and what I dreaded has happened to me" (Job 3:25).

Fear is like a magnet, it will attract into your life exactly what you dread. Job said, "*The thing I greatly feared*", when nothing had even happened yet. This fear haunted his mind with the threat that it could come true, making him suffer over and over again as if what he feared was already happening to him. Let›s look at the context or the circumstances surrounding this event. According to Scripture, Job was one of the patriarchs, a perfect man, upright, God-fearing, and turned away from evil.

These are the characteristics God uses to describe him. Before the coming of Jesus Christ, sins were expiated through the sacrifice of animals. Out of fear of losing his goods, family, or getting sick, Job offered burnt offerings to God. If his children had sinned, they could be forgiven and nothing bad would happen to them. However, what he feared happened to him just as he imagined. No other adverse situations happened to him, but those he dreaded. That's how powerful fear is. Fear is like a delusion; you can't see it, but believing it will happen can fill your life with isolation and madness. Like the feeling of being chased when no one is really chasing you. Because you think you´re being chased, you run to hide or walk faster, but when you turn to look there is no one there.

Why are we afraid? I will begin with a brief testimony: Some time ago, I was in a family's home helping them in their walk with God. One night while I was sleeping, I heard a very clear and powerful voice that told me, "You don't have anyone, no one wants you." Although I was sound asleep, I felt as if a dagger had plunged into my heart and I began to cry. I cried for a few seconds with great intensity and realized I had woken from my sleep. I said to that voice, "I have the Father, the Son and the Holy Spirit." Immediately this presence left the room. Although all of this happened in a matter of seconds, I felt a physical pain in my chest that lasted the whole morning.

One of Satan's tasks is to sow in your mind that no one loves you, that you don't have anyone, and that you are alone. He begins to plant these thoughts from the moment you are in your mother's womb so that fear takes hold of you.

If the enemy manages to convince you with his arguments, you´ll feel a dagger in your chest that never stops hurting. The wound of heartbreak will begin to ooze pain and fear will become like a host. Those circumstances that frighten you will come and you will act based on fear. For example, if you think that no one loves you, you will look for someone to love you and you'll begin to allow other things into your life.

Love comes from the Father. If you don't have the revelation of God's fatherhood, you will look to the world and the pleasures it offers, which are merely imitations that are led by Satan. Lust is a demonic spirit whose assignment is to imitate true love. It makes you feel pleasure where there is heartbreak. It elevates you then drags you down, making the fall worse than the rise because of the transgression. Then you start looking to men or women for the affirmation you never had. For this reason, children are often initiated into sexual acts or pornography as the perpetrators tell them that this is love. In such a way that if a child grows up lacking in love, they will easily fall into this delusion and will be tied to the temporary satisfaction that this substitute for love produces. This is the reason for infidelity and the sins that tie people's lives to illicit sexual acts. The need to love and be loved is so great that you allow yourself to be carried away by these temptations.

Because children with these deficiencies are often left behind, lonely and sad, they find this "opportunity" and fall into the trap. When the child becomes an adult but has not healed the wound from their childhood, they begin to engage in different relationships waiting to feel loved. Clearly, that is not perfect love. No person can provide it, only the Father. After a while, the heart begins to ache again because the expectation was not fulfilled adequately. The Word of God confirms it:

"Do not love the world or the things in the world. If anyone loves the world, the love of the Father is not in him" (1 John 2:15).

What is the world and what are the things in it? The world is ruled by lust, which is not only sexual sin, but represents everything in which the flesh and the soul find pleasure. The Word of God speaks in detail about it in the following passage:

"For all that is in the world—the lust of the flesh, the lust of the eyes, and the pride of life—is not of the Father but is of the world" (1 John 2:16).

The Word is very specific. Clearly, God is not behind any of these temptations. They are simply options that the devil presents to deceive us, making us believe that with them, we can mitigate the pain caused by heartbreak. In this category are the lusts of the flesh, that is, illicit sexual relations: adultery, fornication, orgies, bestiality, masturbation, perversion, etc. As well as eating disorders in all its meanings: gluttony, obesity, anorexia, bulimia, malnutrition, etc.

I want to make a short parenthesis to share the testimony of a young woman in her thirties, who suffered from morbid obesity, and whom I counseled some time ago. As we discussed her condition, she told me that she had been overweight since she was a child. She recalled that her parents never lived together and she overate because she was very sad. She never received the love of her father. When she was 14 years old he went to see her and told her, "You have to stop eating because nobody likes fat girls". Those words were enough for the teen to become anorexic. She vomited everything she ate, and in her adult life, she became morbidly obese. She was heartbroken and filled with rejection. The wound caused by lack of love produces these types of alterations; the need to be loved and accepted becomes a great pain and can even become an obsession. However, even if your biological father does not meet this need, it is the love of the heavenly Father that really heals your wounds. All of these needs are the desires of the soul simply because the love of the Father is not in a person, as we have seen in Scripture.

Let me continue with the desires of the flesh; vices: drugs, cigarettes, drug addictions, alcohol, sugar, etc.

The lust of the eyes: pornography, greed, envy, etc. Finally, the pride of life: materialism, self-centeredness, selfishness, idolatry, pride, love of money or greed, dishonest profits, conceit, narcissism, boasting, rebellion, independence, insubordination, egotism, self-sufficiency, gambling, etc.

The Holy Scriptures encompass all the temptations in the world into these three categories. The reason for this bondage is that the love of the Father has not been revealed to these hearts. Feeling unloved produces a wound that is incredibly painful to bear. It prompts people to try to fill that void and mitigate the pain with these things.

What the world offers produces death. That is why the expectation of feeling loved through that lifestyle is a big lie. Disobedience will only tie you more to fear:

"And you, He made alive, who were dead in trespasses and sins, in which you once walked according to the course of this world, according to the prince of the power of the air, the spirit who now works in the sons of disobedience, among whom also we all once conducted ourselves in the lusts of our flesh,

fulfilling the desires of the flesh and of the mind, and were by nature children of wrath, just as the others" (Ephesians 2:1-3).

This is a strong statement! We already know that there is a broken heart behind this. We saw that the love of the Father is not in the person who loves the world. But here we find another fatherhood when he says *"sons of disobedience."* He is referring to the devil´s fatherhood and these are the actions of someone who lives under that fatherhood. Loving the world shows that there is orphanhood in a person because he has a fatherhood contrary to that of God´s. The person›s actions show who governs their life, just as Christ told the Jews who boasted assuring that they were children of Abraham. Jesus said to them, *"You are of your father the devil, and the desires of your father you want to do"* (John 8:44a). The great truth is that everyone who is tied to this fatherhood needs the true love of the Father to be revealed to him.

Let's go back to fear. This is not just a feeling, but a demonic entity, a spirit that works in people's lives through cowardice and slavery, which is why Scripture says:

"For God has not given us a spirit of fear, but of power and of love and of a sound mind" (2 Timothy 1:7).

Fear´s intention is to turn the person into a coward because cowards lack courage. As the coward is running, they turn around to see who is chasing them; but the brave man is like a lion, as it says in 2 Samuel 17:10a: *"And even he who is valiant, whose heart is like the heart of a lion..."*.

This bravery analogy associates the brave man's heart with a lion: *"A lion, which is mighty among beasts and does not turn away from any"* (Proverbs 30:30).

Fear not only makes you turn around but also paralyzes you. It is so strong that the Lord counteracts it with power, love, and self-control. Since it was not God who gave you cowardice, you have to consciously reject it. Now, if you didn't receive it from God, who sent it? Satan!

Scripture points out that there is punishment in the heart of those who fear:

"There is no fear in love; but perfect love casts out fear, because fear involves torment. But he who fears has not been made perfect in love" (1 John 4:18).

This is the punishment we see in Job's heart when he mentions the dread that frightened him. In other words, it tormented him and made him suffer as if what he feared was happening to him. That is punishment, the scourge of believing that something unreal is real. Fear is linked to the absence of love. Not being perfected in this love can mean that you do not know Him, because God is love and the one who fears has not been perfected in love. The love of the Father is the only love that can remove all of those roots of fear that are within us. Of course, a human being´s first appreciation of love is from their earthly parents, like the love your mom gave you when you were in the womb and then the love your dad gave you. However, we know that many babies are conceived in sin; I am referring to fornication, which is sexual relations outside of marriage, or adultery, which is sexual relations in which one or both are married to another person.

There are also many terrible situations such as rape under the influence of alcohol, orgies and all those sinful relationships included in the Word of God. These situations cause the baby to generate fear because of sin, as Scripture indicates in chapter three of Genesis. This is the first time fear or dread is mentioned in the Holy Scriptures; it's no wonder this chapter is called: "The disobedience of man." God put Adam and Eve in the Garden of Eden and told them that they could eat the fruit of every tree, except the fruit of the tree of the knowledge of good and evil. But Scripture tells us that because the serpent was cunning, he deceived Eve. He told her that if she ate this fruit she would not die but that her eyes would be opened and they would be like God, knowing good and evil. So she ate and gave the fruit to her husband as well. Exactly as Satan had told her, it happened; their eyes were opened and they became aware that they were naked. Textually the Scripture says:

"And they heard the sound of the Lord God walking in the garden in the cool of the day, and Adam and his wife hid themselves from the presence of the Lord God among the trees of the garden. Then the Lord God called to Adam and said to him, 'Where are you?'So he said, 'I heard Your voice in the garden, and I was afraid because I was naked; and I hid myself.' And He said, 'Who told you that you were naked? Have you eaten from the tree of which I commanded you that you should not eat?' Then the man said, 'The woman whom You gave to be with me, she gave me of the tree, and I ate'" (Genesis 3:8-12).

If you have young children you know what they know. When they come home after school and say a word you´ve never heard them say before or talk about something you didn't teach them, at once you understand that someone has intervened in their mind. This is what happened with Adam. When he told the Father that he was afraid and that was why they were hiding, God knew that someone had intervened and that Adam had done exactly what He told him not to do. He knew it because He is the Father.

The sin of disobedience brought fear into the lives of human beings. When a baby is conceived in rebellious or disobedient conditions, fear will enter the womb and will begin to try to convince that little one that no one wants them, that it is better not to come out. This also happens in the case of births where they use forceps. Troubled homes where there is yelling, cursing, abuse, and vices, will affect the baby and fill them with fear. Lack of knowledge makes us slaves to fear. A sense of fear can easily grow in the baby without the mother or father even needing to tell them, "I don't love you", when they are in the womb. Satan will do it with the right he has because of the sin. In addition, there are many cases in which some children are rejected by their parents from pregnancy. Babies have the ability to hear and perceive love, this means that from conception the baby is expectantly waiting for their parents´ loving response or rejection. Love is a basic and fundamental need.

The **love of the Father** is the only love that

can **remove** all of those roots of fear that are within us.

The wound caused by a lack of love occurs in the heart. It's like having a deep pain in the soul and a great need to be loved. You begin to wander through life looking for someone to love you and this emptiness drives you to become a beggar for love. You are like someone with a love disability, unable to receive it or give it. Time goes by until rebellion and anger arrive due to the lack of love. All of this is accompanied by thoughts of loneliness and voices that tell you: "Nobody loves you." "You are alone." "You are useless." "You don't do anything right." "You're ugly." "You're worth nothing." "You're not going to make it." "That's not for you." "You don't deserve that." Then, depression and sadness begin to grow. This is the pain caused by a lack of love. Why does this lack produce fear? Because you feel that there is no one there to protect you, that the world is against you and that you are too small to overcome it.

In addition to being conceived this way, maybe you grew up in an orphanage, boarding school or in a dysfunctional family where your parents didn't treat each other with love, there were no hugs or kisses, and your siblings offended, assaulted, mistreated, and disqualified you with words. All of this creates a mark on your heart and becomes your inner voice. When difficulty comes, you have nothing to hold on to. You don't have any kind of affirmation or safe place to take refuge emotionally.

There are many types of fears. Job was afraid to lose his property, family, etc., but other people fear being rejected, alone, or hurt, so their heart turns to stone in attempts to avoid this and protect themselves. People are also afraid of death because its transcendental nature between physical and eternal life produces an intense fear. This is what the patient feels when they hear the doctor say, "You have cancer." Upon hearing these words, fear can flood the heart of the one lacking fatherhood. But the Word of God says:

"And again: 'I will put My trust in Him.' And again: 'Here am I and the children whom God has given Me.' Inasmuch then as the children have partaken of flesh and blood, He Himself likewise shared in the same, that through death He might destroy him who had the power of death, that is, the devil, and release those who through fear of death were all their lifetime subject to bondage" (Hebrews 2:13-15).

Scripture is talking about how Jesus Christ overcame death to take away its power. He defeated death and the devil, and with that victory, He freed the children of God from the fear of death. If you´re not a child of God yet because you haven't received Jesus Christ in your heart or you´re a Christian who still does not have the revelation of God's fatherhood, you will be afraid of dying because this freedom is only available to sons and daughters. Again, here we see the relationship with slavery since Jesus freed us from the fear of death and from the bondage this terror imposes on mankind. For God's children, dying is gain, according to the words of the Apostle Paul:

"For to me, to live is Christ, and to die is gain" (Philippians 1:21).

To die is to return home. When you're a child of God this is an essential longing in your heart. We came from the Father and we will return to Him. The theme of slavery, which we will study in chapter five, also contributes to fear operating in people's lives:

"For you did not receive the spirit of bondage again to fear, but you received the Spirit of adoption by whom we cry out, ´Abba, Father´" (Romans 8:15).

This is God the Father´s great answer to humanity: adoption. Identity as God´s sons and daughters is the only thing that can free us from slavery, cowardice, and fear, and heal the wound caused by fear, rejection, and lack of love. The word *Abba* cited in this Scripture means *father.* But it is a word that was used when there was closeness and affection, like when a child calls their dad, "Daddy". The first time the word is mentioned in Scripture, it was spoken by Jesus Christ because of His identity as the Son of God. That is why He was able to reveal this close and filial relationship to the world.

When you receive His adoption, many truths are revealed to you; the greatest of these is that you become aware of the Father's love.

Let's see what this adoption consists of and how it is related to love:

"Behold what manner of love the Father has bestowed on us, that we should be called children of God! Therefore the world does not know us, because it did not know Him" (1 John 3:1).

God's love manifests its power. It's not like any biological father, neither those of good deeds nor those of bad deeds. The love of the Father *has* taken care of His children, it is not absent. The reason for adopting us as His children is simply love. This is the truth of adoption. We live as beggars for love, ignoring this reality, perhaps suffering because our biological father rejected us or offended us, or because the person to whom we offered our hearts belittled us. But the Father has His arms wide open and is offering us His love and the possibility to be called His children to enjoy all of His tenderness, protection, and inheritance. It's like having a treasure but not knowing it is available to you, therefore, suffering the need of not having it, nevertheless:

"In this is love, not that we loved God, but that He loved us and sent His Son to be the propitiation for our sins" (1 John 4:10).

Not only has God loved us without us doing anything to deserve it, but He sent His Son so that we may be free from fear, lack of love and everything in the world. When He says He has adopted and liberated us, He means that He has given us of His Spirit:

"By this we know that we abide in Him, and He in us, because He has given us of His Spirit. And we have seen and tes-

tify that the Father has sent the Son as Savior of the world. Whoever confesses that Jesus is the Son of God, God abides in him, and he in God. And we have known and believed the love that God has for us. God is love, and he who abides in love abides in God, and God in him. Love has been perfected among us in this: that we may have boldness in the day of judgment; because as He is, so are we in this world" (1 John 4:13-17).

Jesus Christ is the door through which we must enter to enjoy this never-ending love. We have a wonderful deposit of love if we abide in Him. The Spirit quickens, heals, and raises us from the dead. Notice how John calls Jesus *"The Savior of the world."* Although we are in the world, we do not love what this world loves because we´ve been saved and freed from it to be as this passage says, "*as He is, so are we in this world.*" We are in this world as Jesus Christ is: loved! Just as the Father said to Jesus when in an act of obedience He was baptized and came out of the waters:

"Then a voice came from heaven, ´You are My beloved Son, in whom I am well pleased´" (Mark 1:11).

Just as Jesus is to the Father: loved and worthy of all His pleasure, *so are we in this world.*

I want to emphasize two more things in 1 John 1: *"And we have* ***known*** *and* ***believed*** *the love that God has for us"* (1 John 4:16a).

It's not enough to know this love through His Word or to receive Jesus Christ as Savior, it is necessary for us to believe in this love, because it literally says, *" that we may have* ***boldness****"* (1 John 4:17a).

Furthermore, the person who has fear in their heart has a hard time trusting others. The truth is, the untrusting person tries to protect themself from getting hurt. They don´t let others into their life easily and have superficial relationships based on hypocrisy. Why is it so difficult for human beings to believe that they are loved? For all the reasons we´ve discussed. Our belief system must be based on something because we´ve been designed by God with the ability to believe, so there can be no gaps. I will either believe that I am loved or I will believe that I am not loved. The correct belief will bring confidence into my life, the wrong one, fear.

I will share a couple of testimonies to dive deeper into the subject. From the time I was a child to right before I met my heavenly Father, I defended myself from the rejection that my sisters and mother exerted on me with this idea: "They do not love me, but my father does", referring to my biological father. I did this for many years and even used it in every one of my relationships. This thought was based on the relationship I had with my father. I used this argument as a crutch to go to university, get my first job, travel, etc. When fear or rejection appeared, I leaned on this predominant thought that I had. However, this kind of love was insufficient for me. Parents love with weaknesses, like all human beings, and only when I knew the truth -- that I will tell you about next -- was that I experienced perfect love.

One day, I was interceding for a pastor who had shared from the pulpit that witches were attacking him to disintegrate the church. I had no idea how much this experience would help me. As he spoke on the subject, I sensed the fear in his words, he spoke as one who felt unprotected. When I prayed for him, I visualized him in his childhood and saw that he was hurt by his father. He cried a lot while because he was mistreated and I could discern the orphanhood in his heart. God told me to let go of the defense I had used with my biological father and to elevate the trust I had put in him to His love. Then He led me to this verse that is the most valuable revelation the heavenly Father has given me against fear:

"Nevertheless the Lord your God would not listen to Balaam, but the Lord your God turned the curse into a blessing for you, because the Lord your God loves you" (Deuteronomy 23:5).

Balaam was a prophet. The enemies of God's people had hired him to curse Israel. However, the explanation given by Scripture of his frustrated attempt is: *"because the Lord your God loves you"*. This is the powerful reason why Satan cannot touch you or curse you. But as we saw in the previous verse, the requirement is that you must believe in this love. It can be very difficult to understand that the heavenly Father loves you if you´ve had an abusive or absent father because you will relate the love of God to the one you received from your biological father. But regardless of whether you were loved or rejected by him, you must forgive him and raise your belief system to the level of Scripture because you will become what you believe.

"For as he thinks in his heart, so is he" (Proverbs 23:7a).

What you believe becomes your source of power. If you believe that no one loves you, it will be fear, but if you believe that God loves you, it will be trust and confidence. This passage is very impactful. The reason so many people are frustrated is because they have not been able to fulfill their purpose. Fear will do its best to introduce into the mind of the human being that they are unprotected, helpless, and that no one defends them. That's what I felt when I lost my father; that I was left alone and that no one was in my favor. Logically, that was not true because the love of the heavenly Father is always within our reach.

"When I cry out to You, then my enemies will turn back; ***This I know, because God is for me****"* (Psalm 56:9).

Confirm your trust in Him:

"He will not be afraid of evil tidings; His heart is steadfast, trusting in the Lord'" (Psalm 112:7).

"The Lord is on my side; I will not fear. What can man do to me?" (Psalm 118:6).

The confidence the psalmist had can only be a reality in the heart that has believed and known the love of the heavenly Father. Orphanhood produces a feeling of forsakenness and being unprotected during which the person feels completely vulnerable and exposed to the attacks of the enemy and the people he uses. But the truth is that the heavenly Father's love is a powerful force in the spiritual world; it is a shield against the attacks of the devil! No one can do anything against you, only what the Father has determined. Let's look at Jesus' response to Satan's attempt to terrorize Him.

According to the following passage, Jesus is going to be arrested and taken before the authorities to be crucified. In an attempt to defend Jesus, one of His disciples strikes a servant of the High Priest and cuts off his ear. Faced with this defensive reaction, Jesus replied:

"Or do you think that I cannot now pray to My Father, and He will provide Me with more than twelve legions of angels? How then could the Scriptures be fulfilled, that it must happen thus?" (Matthew 26:53-54).

As you can see, the enemy cannot do more than the Father allows him. Jesus´ conviction that His Father would send Him more than 12 legions of angels if He cried out is the same that you and I, as children of God, must have. Jesus spoke about what He believed in His heart about His Father´s love and protection.

Let's look at other Scriptures on this emphasis:

"Therefore My Father loves Me, because I lay down My life that I may take it again. No one takes it from Me, but I lay it down of Myself. I have power to lay it down, and I have power to take it again. This command I have received from My Father" (John 10:17-18).

This is the same confidence that we have when the love of the Father is in us. No one will be able to take our lives because the Father's love will be our shield. Let's see the answer that Jesus gave to Pilate before He was sentenced to death:

"Then Pilate said to Him, 'Are You not speaking to me? Do You not know that I have power to crucify You, and power to release You?' Jesus answered, 'You could have no power at all against Me unless it had been given you from above. Therefore the one who delivered Me to you has the greater sin'" (John 19:10-11).

This is the identity of a son, Jesus knew very well that no one could touch Him because He was fulfilling what the Father had entrusted to Him. He knew Satan was not sovereign over His life, but actually used to carry out the eternal plans that God had for humanity:

"We know that whoever is born of God does not sin; but he who has been born of God keeps himself, and the wicked one does not touch him" (1 John 5:18).

If you do not have the identity of a child of God, you will be afraid of everything that happens around you. But when you are born of God, the evil one will not be able to touch you. The love of the Father is the most powerful revelation against the spirit of fear:

"For whom He foreknew, He also predestined to be conformed to the image of His Son, that He might be the firstborn among many brethren" (Romans 8:29).

You have been predestined by God to be His son or daughter; and a brother or sister to Jesus Christ.

"Who shall separate us from the love of Christ? Shall tribulation, or distress, or persecution, or famine, or nakedness, or peril, or sword?" (Romans 8:35).

"Yet in all these things we are more than conquerors through Him who loved us. For I am persuaded that neither death nor life, nor angels nor principalities nor powers, nor things present nor things to come, nor height nor depth, nor any other created thing, shall be able to separate us from the love of God which is in Christ Jesus our Lord" (Romans 8:37-39).

The Holy Scriptures make it very clear that there is nothing that can separate us from the love of God. The Creator loves us and He is our Father. Therefore, what was created does not have the power to separate us from this love, unless you and I reject it or exchange this love for fear and decide to believe that we are alone. We are like Christ in this world, loved by the Father. The chapter on the preeminence of love focuses on the significance of God's love. This passage of Scripture emphasizes the importance of being loved and loving, and it is for this reason that the wound is so painful and deep:

"And though I have the gift of prophecy, and understand all mysteries and all knowledge, and though I have all faith, so that I could remove mountains, but have not love, I am nothing" (1 Corinthians 13:2).

Notice that he doesn't say, "I have nothing", but, "I am nothing." The absence of love robs us of our identity as children of God. This is the reason we try to love the world through the lust of the eyes, the lust of the flesh, and the pride of life.

The love of money and everything else says that you need to have something to be someone, but that's a big lie! We are because the Father loves us.

"For now we see in a mirror, dimly, but then face to face. Now I know in part, but then I shall know just as I also am known. And now abide faith, hope, love, these three; but the greatest of these is love" (1 Corinthians 13:12-13).

We will talk about the phrase *"face to face"* in chapter seven corresponding to glory. However, let's think about the expression, *"Then I shall know just as I also am known"*. *Knowing* is a word used to refer to intimacy. This is the revelation of the Father's love since I was known beforehand in His love and predestined to be loved by Him. This is why the greatest of these, faith, hope, and love, is love. I reiterate: God's love is your shield against fear and lack of protection; you are a child of God and you are loved. *"And now abide faith, hope, love, these three; but the greatest of these is love"*; love is what activates faith. This is why it's so difficult to believe in God. The wound produced by lack of love causes orphanhood. This makes people afraid and fear prevents them from believing.

"For in Christ Jesus neither circumcision nor uncircumci-

sion avails anything, but faith working through love" (Galatians 5:6).

"Having predestined us to adoption as sons by Jesus Christ to Himself, according to the good pleasure of His will, to the praise of the glory of His grace, by which He made us accepted in the Beloved. In Him we have redemption through His blood, the forgiveness of sins, according to the riches of His grace" (Ephesians 1:5-7).

When you have this truth in your heart and you believe it, you don't need to look for more love because you already have it. God's fatherhood ends the orphanhood that is linked to fear and rejection. No one can hurt or reject you, you are *accepted in the Beloved.* You are a child of God and you are loved.

Let's look at another area related to fatherhood and the love of God. Religion in all its manifestations has generated terror or fear of God in people. The truth is that there is indeed a reverence or respect for the heavenly Father, but in no way should that translate to fear. The Scripture, referring to Jesus says:

"Who, in the days of His flesh, when He had offered up prayers and supplications, with vehement cries and tears to Him who was able to save Him from death, and was heard because of His godly fear" (Hebrews 5:7).

How are we to relate to the heavenly Father? He is Holy, so we should approach God with reverent fear, humility, and meekness, not with demands or resentment. Notice that Scripture makes a very clear point that Christ was the *Son*. Now, being a son or daughter should not be understood that we will be exempt from processes of formation, trials, or the Father´s discipline to lovingly teach us. We are to have the assurance that He will always be with us.

God's fatherhood loves and disciplines:

"And you have forgotten the exhortation which speaks to you as to sons: ´My son, do not despise the chastening of the Lord, nor be discouraged when you are rebuked by Him; For whom the Lord loves He chastens, and scourges every son whom He receives.´ If you endure chastening, God deals with you as with sons; for what son is there whom a father does not chasten? But if you are without chastening, of which all have become partakers, then you are illegitimate and not sons" (Hebrews 12:5-8).

As we´ve learned, Christ is our example in everything. Scripture says about Him, *"Because of what He suffered, He learned obedience."* This is really the fatherhood of God in a person's life; His love includes discipline and scourge for all those He receives as sons and daughters. Such discipline is a problem for many people because of the distorted image they have of God due to the treatment they received from their biological parents. Some think that God is extremely forgiving and that He will not be harsh with reprimand, but others believe that God is a tyrant and abuser. However, His discipline comes upon us because He is a loving Father.

On the other hand, children who´ve been raised in a disrespectful way or who resist authority have a profound absence of love. Resisting authority can eventually land them in jail because they are unable to submit. These are the people whom the Lord calls *illegitimate children.* We must have a fair understanding of God's fatherhood and His discipline, the origin of which is His love. Now, this is how Scripture describes illegitimate children:

"One of illegitimate birth shall not enter the assembly of the Lord; even to the tenth generation none of his descendants shall enter the assembly of the Lord" (Deuteronomy 23:2).

These illegitimate children are usually very rebellious, violent, irreverent, and explosive in their reactions. Their character is inspired by their father´s rejection and their sinful conception, which means they were conceived illegitimately or outside the marriage covenant. It is very difficult for them to understand that discipline is a manifestation of love. These people find it difficult to recognize God as Father because any kind of father figure triggers anger and resentment in them. Their hearts are filled with fear. They are in the house of God or wander from one place to another, but when rules are enforced, they leave. In the same way, they have problems with justice and people in positions of authority. Finally, let us note that Deuteronomy 23:2 says it's a curse since it is established for ten generations.

Let's go back to the topic of sons and daughters, there are children who have idolized their earthly parents. They want to be just like them; in fact, the child always looks for a figure they can admire to imitate, be it a stepfather, an uncle, a grandfather, etc. Let's see what else the Word says about love and discipline:

"Furthermore, we have had human fathers who corrected us, and we paid them respect. Shall we not much more readily be in subjection to the Father of spirits and live? For they indeed for a few days chastened us as seemed best to them, but He for our profit, that we may be partakers of His holiness" (Hebrews 12:9-10).

How many people imitate their parents´ behavior? Many times, even though such behavior goes against God's will, they "worship" their parents and resist God's discipline because their parents did it differently. In the previous verse, God says it is better to accept His discipline so that we can live! And He concludes with the following:

"Now no chastening seems to be joyful for the present, but painful; nevertheless, afterward it yields the peaceable fruit of righteousness to those who have been trained by it" (Hebrews 12:11).

Ultimately, God's discipline is only for His beloved children. The times of scourging are not pleasant, but they will produce the fruit of righteousness as received by Jesus Christ. This benefit is also a manifestation of the Father's love.

If you are loved, you will be disciplined.

Prayer to receive God's Fatherhood and Love

(Fear)

Heavenly Father, I come before You. I ask that You grant me to be strengthened with power in my inner man by Your Spirit. I ask You to forgive me for looking for love in other sources instead of coming to You. Forgive me for looking at what the world offers to fill the emptiness caused by the lack of love and rejection I experienced.

I ask You to forgive me because I have sinned against You, I believed the lies of Satan and I denied the faith. Forgive me because I have harbored unbelief in my heart, believing that I am alone and unprotected, and that You do not love me. Your Word says that everything that does not come from faith is sin, so today I confess my transgression before You and I repent. Your Word also says that if we confess our sin You are faithful and just to forgive and cleanse us from all wrongdoing, thank You.

I ask Your forgiveness for my parents´ sin and because they conceived me in sin. I repent for them and for my grandparents, great-grandparents, and great-great-grandparents, because we have all sinned against You and because our disobedience gave fear access to our lives. Today I make the decision to break the agreement that I made, consciously or unconsciously, with the spirit of cowardice and fear. I renounce these demons and cast out every unclean spirit that entered my life from my mother's womb to cause fear and rejection. I forgive my parents for conceiving me in sin, and cast out every unclean spirit of unbelief, lies and doubt.

I bless my parents and I thank You for choosing them to give me life, because without them I would not exist. I love and accept the parents You gave me in Your sovereignty. I confess and believe that God is my heavenly Father, and that He loves me deeply. I am His child and worthy of His protection, love, care, provision, inheritance, power, and eternal life.

Father, through faith, I receive Christ in my heart so that rooted and grounded in His love, I may be fully capable of understanding what is the width, the length, the depth and the height of His love. And in knowing the love of Christ that exceeds all knowledge, I will be filled with all your fullness.

Holy Spirit, I love You, come and dwell in me. I receive You in my life and thank You for filling me with power, love, and self-control. Through faith, I accept and receive the love of my heavenly Father; I make the decision that I will never be afraid again because my Father's love is my shield. His angels protect me and encamp around me and no one can reject me or hurt me because I am accepted by my Father who loves me and made me His child. I will not fear bad news, I will not fear what man can do to me, I will not fear death because my Father is my keeper and His power is in me.

The perfect love of my Father casts all fear out of me. My Father loves me just as I am because His hands shaped me. He delights in me and created me to love me. Thank You Father for loving me! I reconcile myself to Your love, I believe it. My heart is filled with joy to know through Your Word that I am loved. I respond to Your love, in the name of Jesus Christ.
Amen.

Chapter 3

Fatherhood and Grace
(Condemnation/Works)

Perhaps we have an accusing past or a present that points out the evil in our deeds. How many of us have felt unworthy of getting closer to God because of it? When something bad happens, your conscience immediately blurts out, "You deserve it" or "This happens to you because of ...," and reminds you of something you´ve done.

The parent's voice, and many times that of the siblings, becomes a person's inner voice. It can constantly tell you, "You're bad," "You're a liar," "That's why nobody loves you," "You're a mess," "You're mediocre," "You're unstable." So when something goes wrong, that's the voice you hear inside of you. Well, that's your identity.

Children's self-esteem is formed by what their parents, siblings, or environment tell them. This can accompany them for the rest of their lives. It is also the reason why they build a wrong image of who God is, it stems from a distorted perception of themselves.

Condemnation is like a prison within us, it is a mental state of constant guilt. The human being has the implicit capacity to know good and bad. The Word of God says that even Creation testifies of the existence of God, however, sin darkens our mental clarity. Because sin separates us from God, we feel like His enemies and our own conscience accuses us, telling us that we are far from him.

Scripture confirms it:

"*For if when we were enemies we were reconciled to God through the death of His Son, much more, having been*" (Romans 5:10).

This is the condition of a person who feels condemned when they are an enemy of God. Let's look at another passage:

"*He who is not with Me is against Me, and he who does not gather with Me scatters*" (Luke 11:23).

Not being at peace with God turns us against Him and that's when guilt rises.

Not knowing Jesus Christ, or if knowing Him you decide not to believe, condemns you. The soul has the capacity of storing memories by categories; you could know Jesus Christ as Savior and Lord and have financial freedom, but still feel condemned for an abortion that you have not been able to forgive yourself for. And if faced with the inability to have a baby, which you now want, you could easily think, "This is punishment for what I did." Not allowing Jesus to redeem an area of your life will keep you under condemnation.

"*He who believes in Him is not condemned; but he who does not believe is condemned already, because he has not believed in the name of the only begotten Son of God*" (John 3:18).

To be an enemy of God, to be against Him, and ultimately to be under condemnation is man´s condition without Him since not believing in God's forgiveness condemns.

The world has taught us its own reward system. From a very young age, children are taught that if they behave well they will be rewarded, and if they misbehave, they are told that they do not deserve the reward. So man has become accustomed, as the popular expression goes, to "making a living." But, biblically speaking, this is a system of works; to be rewarded based on conduct or on one's own merit. This is part of the curse caused by Adam's disobedience and for falling from the position where the Father had placed him in the Garden of Eden. Just as we learned in the previous chapter, fear entered into play because of man's disobedience. In the same way, there is another consequence. The Father issued the sentence:

"*In the sweat of your face you shall eat bread till you return to the ground,for out of it you were taken;for dust you are, and to dust you shall return*" (Genesis 3:19).

Adam had all the privileges of a son: fellowship, love, protection, and provision, but his disobedience took away his position of authority and the government he exercised over the earth. However, I do not want you to see the Father as a tyrant unable to forgive Adam for his fault. What happens is that the kingdom of heaven is constituted under the law. What I mean is that God told Adam that whoever ate the forbidden fruit would die. That included spiritual death and dividing life in two: the earthly life and the eternal life. Because of the legality, God could not annul His own laws. Although His heart was filled with pain because of the way Satan had deceived Eve causing the fall of Adam, He could not annul the decree He had made over His Creation.

When we ignore the Word of God, the enemy works in our lives through our conscience. This means that he reminds us that we are under a curse and that we must earn our bread with the sweat of our brow, that we are God's enemies, and that we are condemned. For this reason, you´ve heard phrases like, "This is the life I *had* to live!"

Let me explain the Father's magnificent and loving plan designed to reunite with us and set us free from all these dire consequences.

The first thing is that you are not the author of sin, it does not bear your name and it did not enter the earth because of you. If you´ve done something wrong or if you've transgressed God's commandments, it is because of what Adam did. He was the door for sin to enter your life:

"*Therefore, just as through one man sin entered the world, and death through sin, and thus death spread to all men, because all sinned—*" (Romans 5:12).

It is like a big generational chain that connects us to Adam. He was under a curse when humanity began to multiply, so we are all under the curse that Adam received. There are many people who don´t understand the need for a Savior. If you did not have sin you would not need redemption.

I've talked to many people who say, "I'm a good person," "I don't harm anyone," "I help people in need," "I go to church on Sundays," "I give offerings and donate," etc. But doing good works outside of the will of God will not keep them from His judgment. Sin certainly did not enter the world through you, but by entering through Adam it also placed all of us under a curse. The aforementioned works do not make you "a good person" since every person's conscience has its own standard of good and bad. Let us analyze the example of these three fathers: The first mistreated his son by beating him in an extremely violent manner, the second killed his son by poisoning him so that he wouldn´t suffer, and the third mutilated him until he bled to death. Now, if the former heard what the latter did to his son, he would think that he was a good man. At least he didn't kill his son, right? The one who killed his son by poisoning him would say that he is better than the one who mutilated him because he didn't make him suffer. But which of them could really put a standard between good and bad? Only God. Each person's conscience cannot establish the rules of morality because they would be left to the discretion of man. For an African tribe, mutilating part of the body or scarring the face is something cultural. According to them, it could be considered something good. But if an American went on vacation, would it be good to allow them to do the same to him? I don't think so!

Scripture shows that we are all without exception under sin:

"*There is none righteous, no, not one; there is none who understands; there is none who seeks after God. They have all turned aside; they have together become unprofitable; there is none who does good, no, not one*" (Romans 3:10-12).

"*For all have sinned and fall short of the glory of God*" (Romans 3.23).

There is a wicked force at work behind humanity on this issue; an imbalance. There are those who believe they are good people and others who believe they are so bad that they can´t be forgiven even if they are introduced to Jesus. The truth is that we have all fallen short of the glory of God because of the sin that entered humanity through Adam's transgression. This distorts the traditional teaching that many people preach that says, "It's because of me, because of what I did, it's my fault." We´ve been taught so much that it's our fault that our conscience begins to establish a structure of condemnation. We already know that it's Satan's fault, *he* deceived Eve and this incited Adam.

The heavenly Father sent His Son to make atonement for sin. Jesus suffered the wrath of God in order to fulfill the law that required the shedding of blood to forgive and remove sin. That is why John the Baptist calls Him, "the Lamb of God, who takes away the sin of the world."

Through one man, sin entered, but also atonement:

"*Therefore, as through one man's offense judgment came to all men, resulting in condemnation, even so through one Man's righteous act the free gift came to all men, resulting in justification of life. For as by one man's disobedience many were made sinners, so also by one Man's obedience many will be made righteous*" (Romans 5:18,19).

This is like a great love story. The weight of sin was too heavy and only perfect blood could pay such a high price. However, Christ, the gift of God, has been undervalued because of the lack of understanding of the implication this sacrifice has. In the spiritual world, only perfect blood can atone for sin:

"*And according to the law almost all things are purified with blood, and without shedding of blood there is no remission*" (Hebrews 9:22).

In this passage, we see that the blood makes the remission; an act that has the capacity to condemn or forgive sin, and remove the burden of guilt. This is Christ´s participation in relation to sin; He atoned for sin with His blood and thus removed the condemnation that was transmitted to mankind through Adam. It's clear that this is not about man, but about Satan intervening through Adam, and God acting through Christ. We have no participation in this. The devil's strategy is to aim the guilt towards the person to keep them under condemnation, and in turn, enslave them to the system of works so that they try to obtain forgiveness for themself.

What relationship does orphanhood have with works and condemnation? We must start with the relationship a child has had with their biological father since childhood. If the father has given them love, communication, protection, and provision, the child will feel worthy and deserving of that favor because they are used to having the necessary sustenance. However, this is not the common case since what happened with Adam is the same that would later happen with us. Sin was transferred to the point that abandonment, lack of protection, helplessness, and separation was transferred to us. Parents, in the wake of sin, began to disgrace their calling as parents, and many children without parents were required to work to support themselves.

The sense of protection disappeared from the lives of many children, so like Adam, they would have to work for bread with the sweat of their brow. In Latin America, it's very common to hear people say that because they had many siblings and their father left them, they had to work at the age of eight, nine, or ten years old. This does not include all those who were in orphanages and foster families. The point is, society is taught that everything is earned.

The orphan, according to the Word of God, lacks a "helper." So they must meet their needs on their own, a behavior that develops unbelief about God's favor. Many people don't feel comfortable asking for favors for the sole reason that they have not learned to receive, or at least, not for free. If what we see is the shadow of what we can´t see, meaning our biological father is the shadow of our heavenly Father, the favor we receive is a shadow of God's grace. Our understanding and ability to believe depend on what we've established in those bonds. How can I believe that I deserve something without trying if I´ve never had it? How can I imagine that there will be a gift for me under the tree if I don't even have a house?

Hard situations make people tough, with repressed feelings, without aspirations or dreams, and only thinking that they can go as far as they can supply for themselves. But what happens when the demand exceeds them? They are left wandering in the streets. When you depend on yourself and can no longer provide what you need because of illness, poverty, or simply because you´re in a prison of condemnation, you fall into disgrace.

You must learn about God's grace, which means unmerited favor. It means you should not and cannot do anything to earn it. You cannot obtain the grace of the Father through works.

Let's see how the Prodigal Son's brother related to their father. In this parable, the father had two sons, the youngest is known as the Prodigal Son. He asked his father for his inheritance and went to a remote province where he lived recklessly until he had spent all of it. He had an older brother who, seeing the father's mercy toward the Prodigal to restore him, reacted as the Scriptures describes it below:

"And he said to him, 'Your brother has come, and because he has received him safe and sound, your father has killed the fatted calf.' ´But he was angry and would not go in. Therefore his father came out and pleaded with him. So he answered and said to his father, 'Lo, these many years I have been serv-

ing you; I never transgressed your commandment at any time; and yet you never gave me a young goat, that I might make merry with my friends. But as soon as this son of yours came, who has devoured your livelihood with harlots, you killed the fatted calf for him.' 'And he said to him, 'Son, you are always with me, and all that I have is yours. It was right that we should make merry and be glad, for your brother was dead and is alive again, and was lost and is found'" (Luke 15:27-32).

Without a doubt, this son was an orphan. Although he had his father, he did not know him; he was not able to ask him for what he longed for. When he saw that his brother was getting what he wanted, selfishness and anger arose in his heart. Notice how he complained to his father saying that he had served him for years. This son was frustrated in his service, claiming to have done so for years without receiving anything! Do you really think that the father would put him to serve without paying him? That's impossible! Envy for what his brother received reactivated his jealousy and bitterness, which I think were already there before his brother returned. Although the father told him he had always been with him and that everything he had belonged to him, the older brother tried to please the father with his works. He compared his works to his younger brother's because he felt the treatment received had been unfair. However, although the Prodigal Son's heart was full of deceit, he understood that his father would forgive him. The Scripture says that he felt unworthy to be called a son, which clearly shows he didn't have the revelation about his identity as a son. But he knew that the father's grace could restore him. Instead, the older believed he didn't need grace because he deserved it! He served but was unsatisfied because he said he had never disobeyed. He expressed his resentment when he concluded by telling the father that he had not given him anything.

This eldest son was an orphan, a religious son who thought he could win the father's favor by his obedience and works. The system of works is built by directing favor and grace towards you. But this would not be grace if it were given to you by your conduct, as the Word of God says:

"*And if by grace, then it is no longer of works; otherwise grace is no longer grace. But if it is of works, it is no longer grace; otherwise work is no longer work*" (Romans 11:6).

This orphan did not know God's favor. If he longed for something, why didn't he ask the Father for it? He did his work and expected rewards; he expected to be justified by the law that credited him with good service and obedience. All he had to do was cry out to the Father! But to do so, he needed to meet two requirements. First, he needed to have the revelation that he was a son and an heir to everything, as the father told him. Second, he needed to recognize his sinfulness to be able to access justification by faith through Jesus Christ.

The law demands works, grace provides all that is yours by faith. Look at what the Scripture says:

"*Therefore, having been justified by faith, we have peace with God through our Lord Jesus Christ, through whom also we have access by faith into this grace in which we stand, and rejoice in hope of the glory of God*" (Romans 5:1-2).

The only way to have peace with God is through faith in His Son. There is no condemnation or guilt, we don't have to do works because it is an unmerited favor:

"*Being justified freely by His grace through the redemption that is in Christ Jesus, whom God set forth as a propitiation by His blood, through faith, to demonstrate His righteousness, because in His forbearance God had passed over the sins that were previously committed*" (Romans 3:24-25).

The important thing here is that this grace is received by faith, which means to believe. Sometimes we believe that we´re not deserving of anything, that we´ve never received anything for free, and that we must earn everything with the sweat of our brow. This kind of thinking makes it impossible to understand that just by faith in Jesus Christ, we have a heavenly Father who has provided a way to redeem us and reverse the curse that fell on us and Adam. It's like when they offer us something for free and we immediately get suspicious. We doubt and think, "They don't give away something that´s this good..."

The older brother´s haughtiness is more common than many imagine. There are people that have "served" and "obeyed" the gospel for years. But they get jealous when they see that others, who believe in the Son of God and accept God as their Father, are counted as righteous for this act of faith and begin to receive blessings.

"*To demonstrate at the present time His righteousness, that He might be just and the justifier of the one who has faith in Jesus. Where is boasting then? It is excluded. By what law? Of works? No, but by the law of faith*" (Romans 3:26,27).

There is no service, works, or obedience that can bring grace into your life. This is received only by faith in Jesus Christ. Then, the Father forgives, blesses, redeems, justifies, and prospers you as His child.

Now, let's talk about weakness. One day, I was counseling a man who had been an orphan since he was 11 years old. As he cried, he told me, "I don't want to cry, I don't want to be weak." There was great pain in his soul because of the lack of protection he had suffered from the time he was a child. As an orphan, without a father or mother, he lived alone in the streets looking for provision for himself.

Given the little or no grace he had received in his life, he learned to be "strong" and repress his emotions, in addition to living under the system of works to sustain himself. No one had ever shown him favor; however, weakness makes us vulnerable to the grace and need we have as children of God:

"*And He said to me, 'My grace is sufficient for you, for My strength is made perfect in weakness.' Therefore most gladly I will rather boast in my infirmities, that the power of Christ may rest upon me*" (2 Corinthians 12:9).

With these words, God responded to the apostle Paul when he asked Him to remove the thorn he had in his flesh. Our weakness allows the Father to perfect His power through His grace since to be weak is actually to be strong in Him. The world makes us believe that we must be strong in our own strength, but that is another deception. Sons and daughters may be weak because they have someone to support them through grace, but the orphan must be strong because they have to sustain themself.

Sin does not disqualify us before God, quite the contrary:

"*Moreover the law entered that the offense might abound. But where sin abounded, grace abounded much more, so that as sin reigned in death, even so grace might reign through righteousness to eternal life through Jesus Christ our Lord*" (Romans 5:20-21).

We were far from Him, we were orphans, but God has drawn us back to Him:

"*I will call them My people, who were not My people, and her beloved, who was not beloved. And it shall come to pass in the place where it was said to them, 'You are not My people,' there they shall be called sons of the living God*" (Romans 9:25-26).

Many have understood that they are God's people, but not everyone knows that they are also God's children.

When one does not have the revelation of God´s fatherhood, one lives as the Prodigal Son´s older brother, with a heart full of envy and bitterness. In this regard, Scripture establishes:

"*Looking carefully lest anyone fall short of the grace of God; lest any root of bitterness springing up cause trouble, and by this many become defiled*" (Hebrews 12:15).

He didn´t receive it, not because the Father didn't want to bless him, but because of his own bitterness. This was what kept him from grace. Notice that this Scripture says that Esau sold his firstborn birthright. Now, remember that the Prodigal Son's brother was the oldest, that is, his father's firstborn, but he spoke with such resentment that he resembled a beggar.

I was contaminated by this root of bitterness in my early years of faith. A few bitter religious people who had served for years told me that faith was not enough to be blessed. The truth is that because of the relationship I had with my biological father, I always believed that God was good, in fact, I called Him "Father God''. I grew up with the idea that I could achieve whatever I wanted, especially in my finances, since I didn't have the need to work hard because provision had always been supernatural in my life. This was not an issue that worried me. I had love-related wounds and a lot of rejection in my heart, but not anything finance-related. I started my walk of faith because of a very great and painful loss, but not because I was after a financial blessing. I simply said that God was good and that He wanted to bless us, but my sisters persecuted me. Today, I understand that they were after my faith, the ability I had to believe God because they couldn't. One of them, witnessing God's blessings in my life, told me, "God has favorites."

We know this is blasphemy because God is no respecter of persons and provides for all whom He adopts as children. I remember one day a person told me, "It's not by faith." I was surrounded by a few bitter people who contaminated my heart. I began to focus on winning God's favor by doing works and what do you think happened? I fell under a curse and began to accumulate debt. I searched for the iniquity and reason for my new economic situation. I had so much debt that I could not even pay the interest. I had never been in debt before. I especially remember one day because I had to pay the monthly installment of something I owed and I didn't have enough to give my tithes. I cried uncontrollably. I had received so much condemning doctrine that I looked for a pair of gold earrings of mine to sell so that I could give my tithe. I must say that many "teachers" minister condemnation from the pulpits by teaching the people that they will be "cursed with a curse" if they don't tithe. They teach that they must give to receive according to the word that is in Malachi 3:9. That day, when I was praying to bring the tithe to church, I heard the voice of God tell me:

"Who has preceded Me, that I should pay him? Everything under heaven is Mine" (Job 41:11).

When I heard this I knew I had learned my lesson. *Should I give to God for Him to bless me?* But the voice came again and at that moment my eyes filled with tears as the veil fell off. Everything is from God! You can never give Him first, He gave first. Everything is His, including the earrings I had sold to complete the tithe: *"Or who has first given to Him and it shall be repaid to him?" (Romans 11:35).*

No one can ever do anything to earn God's favor because grace is through faith in Jesus Christ, the Lamb of God from before the foundation of the world. From that moment my financial condition began to change. This root of bitterness is evident in all the Christians who've received nothing from the Father because of their unbelief and the legalism of the system of works. There are many hearts, like that of the Prodigal Son's brother, that contaminate others. Satan operates through these people with the sole intention of suppressing God's grace.

The Word of God establishes the following very clearly:

"*Let us therefore come boldly to the throne of grace, that we may obtain mercy and find grace to help in time of need*" (Hebrews 4:16).

It is by the sacrifice of Christ that we can come before the Father *in confidence* and not under a curse or condemnation. Grace is so high that it has a throne, after all, the throne of God is called the "throne of grace." The law seeks to invalidate unmerited favor at all costs. That is why orphanhood plays a (negative) fundamental role. It makes us believe that we don't deserve to appear before this throne and much less *obtain mercy and find grace to help in time of need*, which means receiving the Father's help in time. With this I am not saying that we shouldn´t tithe, what I'm saying is that we shouldn't do it under condemnation and with the threat of the curse. We give because we are grateful and because everything is from the Father. When we give, we are simply showing Him our gratitude for His grace. There's nothing you can give to receive from God, the only requirement is to have faith in His Son, Jesus. Besides, the tithe is only the minimum standard and we already know that grace is superior in everything. Tithing is part of the law, from which we´ve been redeemed and the position under the new covenant is:

"*So let each one give as he purposes in his heart, not grudgingly or of necessity; for God loves a cheerful giver. And God is able to make all grace abound toward you, that you, always having all sufficiency in all things, may have an abundance for every good work*" (2 Corinthians 9:7-8).

We know that under the law, adultery was the physical union between a man and a married woman. Under grace, Jesus says that if you simply lust for her in your heart, you have already committed adultery with her. Grace demands more. The same applies to the tithe. You give according to what you´ve determined in your heart; we give from gratitude and not out of condemnation.

Grace is not just a biblical doctrine; grace is Jesus Christ:

"*Of how much worse punishment, do you suppose, will he be thought worthy who has trampled the Son of God underfoot, counted the blood of the covenant by which he was sanctified a common thing, and insulted the Spirit of grace?*" (Hebrews 10:29).

Who is the Spirit of grace? Jesus Christ! The undeserved favor of God is Jesus Christ Himself. To affront Him is to go back to the law, back to works, back to boasting like the Prodigal´s orphan brother, *"I´ve never disobeyed you, and I´ve served you for years without receiving anything."* If you believe that because of your perfect obedience, tithe, or offerings you will earn the Father›s blessing, you are insulting the person of Jesus. In the same way, many times the orphan does not want to receive favors, not even from God. This grace is so high that no one can get close, the price is too high and no one can pay it. It can only be obtained through faith in Jesus. But this is nothing new; the religious persecute those who are free in faith just like Ishmael did with Isaac. Again, we see two sons. One had the attitude of an orphan and persecuted the son of the promise who was born according to faith:

"*Tell me, you who desire to be under the law, do you not hear the law? For it is written that Abraham had two sons: the one by a bondwoman, the other by a freewoman. But he who was of the bondwoman was born according to the flesh, and he of the freewoman through promise*" (Galatians 4:21-23).

"*Now we, brethren, as Isaac was, are children of promise. But, as he who was born according to the flesh then persecuted him who was born according to the Spirit, even so it is now. Nevertheless what does the Scripture say? ´Cast out the bondwoman and her son, for the son of the bondwoman shall not be heir with the son of the freewoman.´ So then, brethren, we are not children of the bondwoman but of the free*" (Galatians 4:28-31).

This root of bitterness begins to contaminate until it cancels out faith in God's grace. Those who are orphans like the older brother persecute the children of the Father who have faith. Their very appearance testifies that grace is not in them. The curse of having fallen into the hands of the living God for insulting the Spirit of grace and His Son Jesus Christ is evident. It's something that is seen even in the way they dress. Let's read the story about the adulterous woman:

"*Then the scribes and Pharisees brought to Him a woman caught in adultery. And when they had set her in the midst, they said to Him, ´Teacher, his woman was caught in adultery, in the very act. Now Moses, in the law, commanded us that such should be stoned. But what do You say?´ This they said, testing Him, that they might have something of which to accuse Him. But Jesus stooped down and wrote on the ground with His finger, as though He did not hear. So when they continued asking Him, He raised Himself up and said to them, ´He who is without sin among you, let him throw a stone at her first.´ And again He stooped down and wrote on the ground. Then those who heard it, being convicted by their conscience, went out one by one, beginning with the oldest even to the last. And Jesus was left alone, and the woman standing in the midst. When Jesus had raised Himself up and saw no one but the woman, He said to her, ´Woman, where are those accusers of yours? Has no one condemned you?´ She said, ´No one, Lord.´ And Jesus said to her, ´Neither do I condemn you; go and sin no more´*" (John 8:3-11).

The Pharisees demanded that the law be fulfilled in regards to the sin of this adulterous woman, but Jesus gave them an answer worthy of grace: "You want to fulfill the law? First, show me your perfection!" Jesus said, "He who is without sin," with this declaration Jesus awakened their conscience, which plays a leading role. Scripture says that this was what accused them. The guilty conscience of this type of person is the one that demands works. If your works are bad, the sanction established by law must be applied to you. The narrative tells us that they all started walking away, from the oldest to the youngest. It is evident that the elders had lived longer and therefore had a bigger "pending" balance, however, Jesus is grace. In this passage, law and grace meet, as only Jesus and the woman remained on the scene. This is how it is in real life, we only stand before Jesus to repent. He didn't look at the Pharisees, He was crouched down looking at her. I imagine how Jesus looked at her, that gaze of grace. He asked her, "Where are those who accused you?" I just want to say that this is the most that the anti-grace, religious people can do, *accuse*, but they cannot condemn. To condemn is to issue a sentence, a verdict that belongs to the powers of a judge and only Jesus has this power. So when Jesus asked her, she answered that no one had condemned her, and Jesus, as judge, said to her, "Nor do I condemn you." Why did He tell her, "nor do I"? Because although He is the only One who can condemn, He did not come to earth for that. God's Word makes it clear:

"*For God did not send His Son into the world to condemn the world, but that the world through Him might be saved*" (John 3:17).

Without a doubt, these Pharisees sought to nullify the grace that Christ came to bring. Even before dying on the cross, Jesus Himself was grace in the flesh and had the power to forgive sins, heal, bless, and restore. Throughout Jesus´ ministry on earth, the religious people persecuted Him with the intention that He would enforce the law. They could not bear the benevolence of grace.

Religiosity is not in unbelievers, the Scripture says that the Gentiles have no law. Religiosity is the poison that the Pharisees have on their tongue and in their hearts. They are brothers, but sons of the slave. They are false teachers who nullify grace and have guilty consciences. Their guilty conscience is the reason they look to push others out of grace and into the law, getting trapped in their sins. Do you remember the Jews who told the Lord that their father was Abraham? Read Jesus´ response:

"*I know that you are Abraham's descendants, but you seek to kill Me, because My word has no place in you*" (John 8:37).

He doesn't acknowledge them as *children* of Abraham, but as his *descendants*, and He's right. According to the allegory we saw in Galatians, Abraham had two sons. To this day, the spiritual implications between these two brothers remain. One was the son of the slave who represents and does the works of the law for condemnation and death. The other son is of the free woman; he represents grace and does the works of faith for life. The persecution of the Pharisees against Jesus is the same that was manifested by the older brother against the Prodigal Son. It's the same persecution that exists today, its recurring emphasis is: "You have to strive and work hard like me, serve, be obedient. You cannot be blessed just by believing." In the verse, we just read in John, Jesus tells them that they were trying to kill Him, which is what condemnation really seeks to do. It wants to kill you and finish your faith until you blaspheme the name of the Lord because you feel you didn't receive anything, just like the brother of the Prodigal Son. Condemnation wants to make you bitter and contaminate others. The word that found no room in their hearts is *grace*! They demanded the fulfillment of the law, but grace offers salvation by faith. All this comes from orphanhood, the lack of identity as sons and daughters.

Works become debts. If you try to win God's favor, you´re not receiving grace, but a reward for your good behavior:

"*For if Abraham was justified by works, he has something to boast about, but not before God. For what does the Scripture say? ´Abraham believed God, and it was accounted to him for righteousness.´ Now to him who works, the wages are not counted as grace but as debt*" (Romans 4:2-5).

The confrontation between law and grace means that I have to take off the garment of holiness and declare what's really in my heart, but that's difficult to do for those who are religious. The revelation is in the Scripture: the Prodigal Son's older brother was legalistic. He obeyed to be blessed, served to be blessed, had the full inheritance but did not enjoy it. He was a bitter orphan. Why an orphan?

Because if he had understood the revelation of fatherhood, he wouldn't have seen what was given to his brother as unfair. After all, that blessing was also his! But he just ignored it. The Word says that when he saw what had been given to his brother, he became angry and blamed the Father for the sins that his brother had committed.

> No one can ever do anything to **earn God's favor,** because grace is through **faith in Jesus Christ**

The older brother was legalistic and worked hard, but according to himself, he had received nothing! Do you know why he didn't get anything? Because God doesn't share His glory with anyone and if He would have blessed him, the brother would have boasted in his works. For this son, the Father was the problem. This is a common reaction among those who act like this and end up blaspheming against the Father. All these works count as debts and do not produce the expected effect, but rather the opposite. They become a curse to the point of filling the person with poison, bitterness, and frustration. Remember that grace is for the sinner; if in the face of fault I declare myself *impious* and I acknowledge my sin, understanding that I am not made perfect through works, conduct, tithes, and service, then I can see that area of my life is under ungodliness. First, by faith and grace, you need the revelation of the root of iniquity that may exist in the life of a believer. Then, you can do what David did. Like the Prodigal Son, he confessed his sin, *"I have sinned against heaven and against you."* You will return to the Father, He will run to hug you and kiss you. He will kill the fatted calf, give you new sandals, a ring, and a robe.

This is the only demand from God in regards to sin:

"If we confess our sins, He is faithful and just to forgive us our sins and to cleanse us from all unrighteousness" (1 John 1:9).

Confessing sin to receive forgiveness by faith through Jesus Christ is God's only requirement for man, since Jesus Christ fulfilled every one of the Creator´s requirements.

Confession and repentance produce forgiveness:

"He who covers his sins will not prosper, but whoever confesses and forsakes them will have mercy" (Proverbs 28:13).

Besides confessing, we need to turn away from sin, just as Jesus told the adulterous woman, "Go, and sin no more."

Let's look at another manifestation of the grace of Jesus:

"Afterward Jesus found him in the temple, and said to him, ´See, you have been made well. Sin no more, lest a worse thing come upon you´" (John 5:14).

The reason that the person continues to sin, even after confessing, is because they are under condemnation. They don't really believe they´ve been forgiven, but they who confess their sin and receive the grace of forgiveness, through faith, are immediately set free. The Holy Spirit internally convicts a person of sin by also using their conscience, producing sadness that leads to repentance, which is why confessing sin is so painful:

"For godly sorrow produces repentance leading to salvation, not to be regretted; but the sorrow of the world produces death" (2 Corinthians 7:10).

This repentance, or pain, that man feels in his heart when he's committed a sin is produced by God. It's so that the person confesses, repents, parts ways with the sin, and is saved and forgiven. But the "repentance" of the sin that isn´t confessed produces death and condemnation.

In law, this position is called *res judicata*, that is to say, that earthly justice cannot prosecute the same crime twice. The Holy Spirit does not convict anyone twice for the same sin, because if it has already been confessed, forgiveness is a done deal through faith in Christ. Now if the pain continues, the person is under attack from a spirit of condemnation, not from God.

Once the sin is forgiven it is erased from that person's spiritual record. The Word of God says that God remembers sin no more and casts it into the depths of the sea. This is the love of the Father for His children; grace and unmerited favor accessed only by faith. This is what He did with the Prodigal Son who repented; He forgave him and restored him through grace. Faith is counted as righteousness, while unbelief is counted as unrighteousness.

“ ...*for **whatever is not from faith** is sin*” (Romans 14:23c).

These are Jesus´ words to Martha before His religious explanation of Lazarus´ resurrection:

“Jesus said to her, ´Did I not say to you that if you would believe you would see the glory of God?´” (John 11:40).

Only faith can produce the Father’s grace and only a child can believe that the Father will give it to them. The orphan simply looks from a distance but does not come close.

Prayer to receive God´s Fatherhood and Grace

(Condemnation/Works)

Heavenly Father, I confidently come before You. I stand before Your throne of grace and mercy to find grace and timely help through the blood of Jesus Christ. Thank You for the gift of grace and for Your gift of salvation to me. Forgive me for believing that I could obtain Your grace and achieve salvation through my works. Forgive me for insulting the Spirit of grace by rejecting Your redemption. Now I understand that it's not because of what I do or how I act. It comes from You because of Your love and the work of Jesus Christ, who took upon Himself all of my injustices, iniquities, evil, and more so, all the pain and bitterness, in addition to paying the price of my guilt on the cross.

I confess my sins before You and renounce the condemnation that my conscience accuses me of. Today I reconcile myself to You and I believe, by faith, that You've forgiven all my sins. And I believe that You´re not mad at me.

Now I understand that Your seed in me keeps me from sinning and shows me the way I should walk. Father, I ask

Your forgiveness for not obeying Your Holy Spirit when He alerted and exhorted me because I wanted to do my will and not Yours.

Today, I ask You to tune my ears to hear Your voice and that Your Holy Spirit would guide me along paths of justice and righteousness for Your name's sake. Help me renew my mind to know Your good, pleasant, and perfect will for me, even if it doesn't look like it to me at the Moment. Help me not to condemn myself, but go before You with a humble heart and in truth to find forgiveness in You.

Help me to be diligent to read Your word and seek You in the secret place. I want to grow even more in the knowledge of You and understand the fullness of Your love for me. Your grace is what sustains me, I want to embrace it and learn to recognize the difference.

I ask all of this in the name of the Lamb of God who takes away the sin of the world and who is sitting at Your right hand.
Amen.

Chapter 4

Fatherhood and Worship

(Soul tie/Lies)

I want to begin this chapter by talking about the Samaritan Woman. Samaria was a region that was made up of Jews and pagan people. The Samaritans were a mixture of Israelites, Assyrians, and other nations, which is why the Jews hated them. They were familiar with Jacob, he was the son of Isaac of the lineage of Abraham, whom they recognized as their father. But like I shared before, anyone who recognizes someone other than their birth father and our heavenly Father as their father does not have the revelation of fatherhood. They are an orphan in their soul.

This Samaritan woman had a conversation with Jesus. She was surprised when He said to her, "Give me a drink"; He was a Jew and she was a Samaritan and a woman! Because of the custom of the time, she replied,

"How is it that You, being a Jew, ask a drink from me, a Samaritan woman?" (John 4:9).

With His response, the Master tries to bring this woman out of the earthly context in which the story takes place:

"If you knew the gift of God, and who it is who says to you, 'Give Me a drink,' you would have asked Him, and He would have given you living water" (John 4:10).

But this woman did not understand the words of the Lord and continued in the earthly reality, so she replied:

"Sir, You have nothing to draw with, and the well is deep. Where then do You get that living water?" (John 4:11).

And goes on to say:

"Are You greater than our father Jacob, who gave us the well, and drank from it himself, ´as well as his sons and his livestock?´" (John 4:12).

Notice that her first problem was her prejudice towards Jesus because she asks Him if perhaps He is greater than Jacob. She didn't know who was speaking to her, since Jesus is not only greater than Jacob, but the Word made flesh. Furthermore, by calling Jacob her father, we see that her soul is full of orphanhood.

Then Jesus answered her:

"But whoever drinks of the water that I shall give him will never thirst. But the water that I shall give him will become in him a fountain of water springing up into everlasting life" (John 4:14).

What is the meaning of the water in the well? The satiety of the world, temporary satisfaction, and the crutches that help you move forward. But just like Jesus told her, *"Whoever drinks of this water will thirst again."* This thirst is the emptiness that is felt once the temporary desires of sin have wreaked havoc in our lives and the expectations of being satisfied have been uncovered. That is when we understand that they cannot really satisfy us. Jesus says to stop taking from the well of the wrong father and to draw out from the source of the heavenly Father. He is not just the only One that satisfies us, but in Who we find eternal life; Jesus tells her that the water from this fountain is for eternal life. Now the Samaritan Woman begins to understand that there is more depth to Jesus´ words than she had understood. She responds by recognizing Him as Lord:

"Lord, give me this water, that I may not thirst, nor come here to draw" (John 4:15).

What an impressive statement this woman makes! By asking Jesus for water, she was acknowledging that she was thirsty, that every time she drank the water from the well she was thirsty again. Furthermore, she understands that the water the Lord spoke to her about is not from Jacob´s well. She will no longer have to draw it out because the Lord's promise is that a fountain will flow from within her that will keep her satisfied and she will never thirst again! How many Samaritans have I met on my journey with Christ? There are those who know the law and recognize that Jews and Samaritans don't get along; men who do not deal with women; those who recognize others as fathers, be it religious leaders, pastors, or the one who led them to the Scriptures. There are those who, like her, are carried away by sight. Remember she said, "*You have nothing to draw with, and the well is deep.*" But there are also those who upon hearing the words of Jesus, recognize that they are thirsty; they might be unsaved, new believers, or longtime believers. This water that Jesus spoke of is the promise of the Holy Spirit, a topic that I will go into more extensively later. Let's read the following verse from the book of Joel:

"*And it shall come to pass afterward that I will pour out My Spirit on all flesh; Your sons and your daughters shall prophesy, your old men shall dream dreams, your young men shall see visions*" (Joel 2:28).

This promise was fulfilled by God in Acts of the Apostles:

"*And they were all filled with the Holy Spirit and began to speak with other tongues, as the Spirit gave them utterance*" (Acts 2:4).

Having said this, I want to go back to Jesus´ conversation with the Samaritan woman. Faced with the confession of her thirst, she directly asks the Lord for living water and He replies:

"*Go, call your husband, and come here*" (John 4:16).

What does Jesus mean by this? Was this a condition so He would give her a drink? Well, I think that for this promise to be fulfilled in someone's heart, it's necessary to repent and turn to Him, as the Scripture establishes:

"*Repent therefore and be converted, that your sins may be blotted out, so that times of refreshing may come from the presence of the Lord*" (Acts 3:19).

Jesus´ love and grace didn´t point at her or condemn her, He only asked her this question to lead her to repentance; in other words, to draw her to Him and give her a chance. She replied:

"*´I have no husband.´ Jesus said to her, ´You have well said, 'I have no husband,' for you have had five husbands, and the one whom you now have is not your husband; in that you spoke truly´*" (John 17b-18).

When she saw the gift of prophecy, she understood that there´s nothing hidden from Jesus´ eyes. She was glad that she had told Him the truth; she took advantage of the opportunity and spoke the truth in the presence of the Lord. But there's still something left in this passage about Jesus´ prophecy for her, "*For you have had five husbands, and the one whom you now have is not your husband.*" Before knowing the Lord as my Father, this passage was the one I related to the most in all of Scripture. This woman represents a person without identity, who is dependent, who tries to fill the void with men, and seeks affirmation, protection, and shelter. If Jesus told her that the husband she had at that time was not her husband either, it means that this man was someone else´s husband, which made her an adulterous woman. How many women have an adulterous relationship just to feel a man´s care and protection? They do so by enduring humiliation and putting up with unkept promises.

The reason for this wrong, even impious, bond is orphanhood. It is to feel unprotected and lonely, and lacking affirmation, like we saw in the first chapter when we talked about identity. This Samaritan woman was not only unaware of God´s gift, but also believed in a false fatherhood, in Jacob´s. He represents those father figures who cannot sustain or protect you, who make you feel empty and thirsty. This includes mothers who elevate their older sons to the position of a husband. All of these things are like crutches in which there is no eternal life.

Let's continue with this passage to see the importance of Jesus´ words when He told her it was well she had said the truth. What does truth have to do with worship? Let's dive into the relationship between fatherhood and worship. When Jesus´ prophecy about her past and present is revealed, the spirit of prophecy, that is Jesus Himself, convinces her and the revelation of worship emerges:

"*And I fell at his feet to worship him. But he said to me, ´See that you do not do that! I am your fellow servant, and of your brethren who have the testimony of Jesus. Worship God! For the testimony of Jesus is the spirit of prophecy'*" (Revelation 19:10).

The Samaritan woman had a face-to-face encounter with Jesus. He is the testimony and the spirit of prophecy. Worship reveals Jesus, who is the prophecy in Himself. That is why when she said to Him, "*Lord, I perceive that You are a prophet,*" her eyes were opened to worship. So she took advantage of the meeting with the Prophet of prophets to ask Him a question. The dialogue continues:

"*Our fathers worshiped on this mountain, and you Jews say that in Jerusalem is the place where one ought to worship*" (John 4:20).

She asked Him where was the right place to worship, but noticed that now she used the word *fathers*, in plural. This paints worship as an inheritance that was taught by generational tradition, much like the religious inheritances that many of us had but didn't know why we practiced them.

She also highlighted the difference between the Samaritans who worshiped in the mountains located in her region and Jerusalem, where the Jews said was the place to worship. The shocking thing about this question is that they weren't talking about worship, but about the water in the well. But when Jesus revealed Himself to her as a prophet, the question about worship arose and He answered:

"Woman, believe Me, the hour is coming when you will neither on this mountain, nor in Jerusalem, worship the Father" (John 4:21).

This is the first time that Jesus explains to her who really deserves worship: the Father! Why did He tell her the time is coming? Jesus´ response continues:

"You worship what you do not know; we know what we worship, for salvation is of the Jews" (John 4:22).

This context is important because the Samaritan woman, and everything she represents, has several gods, several fathers, and does not know what she worships. But the Jews knew that there was only One God and that the Messiah would come from His people. They also knew that Jerusalem was the epicenter of the Father because that's how He himself had declared it. However, Jesus continues to tell her:

"But the hour is coming, and now is, when the true worshipers will worship the Father in spirit and truth; for the Father is seeking such to worship Him" (John 4:23).

Jesus said to her, *"The hour is coming and now is!"* What does this mean? That the coming of that hour was Him, it was right in front of her. Let›s remember that this story takes place after Jesus left Judea and was on His way to Galilee. However, the Word of God says that it was necessary for Him to pass through Samaria. One day while I was worshiping, I asked the Lord why was it necessary for Him to go through this region. I received the following revelation. Although the shortest route from Judea to Galilee was through Samaria, history tells that the Galileans preferred to take a longer route. They wanted to avoid going through Samaria because of the manifest hatred between these groups of people. The answer that the Lord gave me is that the Samaritans did not know the Father, that is why they called Jacob father. The time had come for them because Jesus Himself is the way to the Father, He is the One who makes this reconciliation possible:

"Jesus said to him, ´I am the way, the truth, and the life. No one comes to the Father except through Me. If you had known Me, you would have known My Father also; and from now on you know Him and have seen Him´" (John 14:6-7).

This is why it was necessary for Jesus to go through Samaria. Later, the Scripture confirms it. Notice the emphasis when Jesus said to her, *"and now is," He* is *the now*! In other words, He is the means and the appropriate time to know the Father! The One who has the water of eternal life was sitting across from her. She worshiped what she didn´t know, so it didn´t depend on where she did it, she simply could not worship God as Revelation 19:10 says. God is the Father and if you don't know this truth; if He is only God or a god to you; if being a believer He is only your Lord, you cannot worship Him as Father. This position assumes that there's a lie in your being, that you do not know who your source is; it's not the five husbands, it's not Jacob, it's not the pastors or leaders. When the soul harbors a lie, it cannot worship. What the Father seeks is not soul-worship, but worship *in spirit and in truth.* That is why to worship, you must first be a son or daughter so that the soul ties would be loosened and the orphanhood wounds healed.

Only an encounter with the gift of God, Jesus Christ, can lead you to this fullness. The soul that sings but is full of lies is not satiated. You need to know that God is your Father because the lie of manipulation and a false fatherhood will only leave you unprotected, will fill you with expectations that can never be met, and emptiness will return. Another great revelation I received from this passage is that the soul can praise, but only the spirit worships.

Only an encounter with the **gift of God,** Jesus Christ, can lead you to this **fullness**

The Father is seeking worshipers *in spirit and in truth.* Let's think about the truth; Jesus said to the woman, *"You told the truth when you said, 'I have no husband'"* (NLV). He was removing the lie that didn't allow her to worship the Father and that separated her from Him. This passage gives special attention to the word "truth" or "true", as He explains that not only had the hour come, but that *true worshipers would worship the Father in spirit and in truth.* Jesus is not just the *way* to the Father, He is also the *truth.* If He told her that the worshipers must be true worshipers, it means that there are false worshipers or ones who lack the truth. So, what's the lie? Ignorance of the Father;

if He is not your Father you will just dance or praise, but you will not be able to worship Him. It is necessary for the lie to be removed. In addition to being true worshipers, He showed her the way they should worship; *in spirit and in truth.* The Father is not worshiped when our soul is bound in lies. Through Jesus, Scripture makes it clear that these are not the worshipers the Father is looking for. Worshipers belong to the Father. You must receive the revelation that He is your Father because the way to worship the Father is *in spirit.* Scripture makes it clear when it says that *God is Spirit.* Because He is not a soul, He must be worshiped in His very essence. It is the spirit of a man who receives the revelation that he is the son of God:

"*The Spirit Himself bears witness with our spirit that we are children of God*" (Romans 8:16).

Orphanhood is deceptive to the soul about who we are and who our Father is. The Spirit is united with the truth:

"*And it is the Spirit who bears witness, because the Spirit is truth*" (1 John 5:6b).

What is the truth that the Spirit of God reveals? What is the truth? Christ Himself! What does this truth speak of? That we are children of God. Take notice of how the Holy Scriptures establish it:

"*The spirit indeed is willing, but the flesh is weak*" (Matthew 26:41b).

The flesh is linked to the soul. We cannot flow in true worship if we don´t do so with the knowledge of fatherhood and in the spirit, since the spirit is connected to the truth. It's the flesh that has an issue with worship. The spirit worships and the soul praises; King David said:

"*Bless the Lord, O my soul; and all that is within me, bless His holy name!*" (Psalms 103:1).

Scripture tells us that we are made up of three areas: spirit, soul, and body:

"*Now may the God of peace Himself sanctify you completely; and may your whole spirit, soul, and body be preserved blameless at the coming of our Lord Jesus Christ*" (1 Thessalonians 5:23).

We can bless the Lord with our being, but only with the spirit can we worship Him. The difference between worship and praise is that worship comes from knowing the Father. We worship God for who He is: the Father! And we praise Him for the wonders He´s done, does, and continues to do. In Psalms we find many references to this:

"*Why are you cast down, O my soul? And why are you disquieted within me? Hope in God, for I shall yet praise Him for the help of His countenance" (Psalms 42:5).*

"Awake, my soul! Awake, harp and lyre! I will awaken the dawn. I will praise you, Lord, among the nations; I will sing of you among the peoples" (Psalms 57:8-9 NIV).

"*My soul shall be satisfied as with marrow and fatness, and my mouth shall praise You with joyful lips*" (Psalms 63:5).

This is one of the Psalms that best describes the reason for praise:

"*I will praise You, **for** I am fearfully and wonderfully made; marvelous are Your works, and that my soul knows very well*" (Psalms 139:14).

The psalmist is in awe of the Creator's works, but where is he convinced of this? In his soul. He says, "*My soul knows very well.*" There´s an impressive connection between praise and the soul, hence the reason why music manages to move a person›s heart even when it does not have any religious content. We were designed so that music stimulates our senses, which are part of the soul, but worship is much more than that. Worship means being satiated in the presence of the Father, receiving direction, being filled; it refers to the flow that comes from the source that Jesus mentioned to the Samaritan woman.

Can an orphan praise God? The answer is yes! I´ve seen worship leaders sing with joy, cry, and groan, but when they step off the altar they feel unprotected and alone, even physically and spiritually sick. So, what's the difference between this so-called worshiper, and the person who goes out for a fun night dancing and singing all night, but when the lights go out, feels empty again? None! Both are without the fatherhood of God and that is emotionalism. Worshiping the Father must fulfill the promise of Jesus: to never thirst again. Only children who´ve received the witness of the Spirit in their spirit that they are children of God can worship. When the Word refers to the Spirit´s *witness*, it means that they´ve been affirmed in their spirit about this truth.

Only sons and daughters can worship. Many praise God for His marvelous works, even an unbeliever can do it since they celebrate when they´ve received some type of blessing. Conversion is not necessary. But being satiated in the presence of the Father is reserved for His children.

Let's move on with this passage in Scripture:

"*...and those who worship Him must worship in spirit and truth*" (John 4: 24b).

Notice the word *must*. Just as Jesus had the need to go through Samaria, so the Father has the need to be worshipped. It's also necessary for each of us to worship the heavenly Father *in spirit and in truth*. We all need a genuine relationship with our Father, with the One who loves us, with the only One who can satisfy us, give us eternal life, and also free us, provide for us, and protect us

Prayer to receive God's Fatherhood and to Worship Him

(Soul ties/Lies)

Heavenly Father, today I come before Your presence confessing my sin. I have worshiped what I did not know; people, goods, other gods, and I've worshiped men as fathers. Please forgive me, I repent.

Today, I recognize before You that I need You and that I am thirsty. I ask that You give me a drink. Grant me the gift of God and satisfy me, Father, with the water from Your source. I never want to thirst again. I renounce the spirit of lies, I renounce the bondage in my soul, I renounce idolatry, I renounce false worship, and I renounce confusion.

Father, today I come before You to worship You as a child, in spirit and in truth. I worship You because You are my Father and I delight in doing so. Satisfy me in Your presence through Your Holy Spirit. Today I ask You to give me to drink, give me living water, give me water that brings eternal life. You are my Source, my God and my Father.

Father, in Your Word You say that You are looking for worshipers who worship in spirit and in truth. I want to be that child who worships You like this, so teach me how to do it, show me how to be a true worshiper. I ask that through my worship the spirit of prophecy would flow into my life.

Today, I surrender to You because I want to decrease and for You to increase in me so that Your Holy Spirit may be the One to cry out "Abba Father" and govern my life.

I don't just want to praise You, I want more, much more. I desire to completely surrender my life and be fully devoted to You so that I can touch Your heart. I ask this in the name of Jesus, the firstborn of all Your children. Thank You because I know that this is Your will therefore I know that You will grant it to me.
Amen.

Chapter 5

Fatherhood and Freedom
(Slavery)

Let's look at the definition of slavery, translated to English from the Royal Academy of the Spanish Language: "Rigorous and strong subjection of the passions and affections of the soul. Excessive restraint by which a person is subjected to another person, a job, or an obligation. Brotherhood or congregation in which several people are enlisted to practice certain devotional acts."

The biblical definition:

Slavery comes from the Greek: *déo*, a primary verb, which means to *bind* (in various applications, literal or figurative), *chain, tie together, arrest, prisoner, hold*".

The Roman slavery system had broad characteristics that express the magnitude of what slavery does to a person. Let's look at the conditions by which one became a slave:

- **Birth:** Children of women who were slaves became slaves of their mother's owner at birth.

- **Conquest:** Enemies captured in the heat of war became slaves.

- **Insolvency:** Debtors faced with an outstanding balance were reduced to slavery by their creditors.

- **Exhibition or sale:** When a baby was born, the father of the family had the right to choose to keep the baby or not. If not, the baby was discarded and taken as a slave or sold as merchandise to pay debts or exchanged in business. This right was called *ius exponendi* and gave the father the power to choose to keep or exhibit the baby. He could take account of the case due to physical defects, illness, not knowing who the father was, or an absolute discretion of the *patér familia*[3].

Sons were called *liber*, unlike slaves. There was a legal figure called *freedmen* and this was the manumission of the masters towards the slaves; this means that they were granted freedom.

---

3 Spanish Strong Concordance 1210

When they were freed, they were given an identity card with their name since slaves did not have identification documents. In this sense, we see that a slave was not considered a person, but merchandise, owned by the master and lacking identity and rights.

The implications that we´ve seen show what human life was reduced to. The definitions that we cited define slavery as submission, binding, or chaining, in a literal and figurative sense by the confinement of the soul to the obedience of others, thus reducing all human passion to the will of the master.

Let's read a quote from Simón Bolívar, who is known as The Liberator and a leading figure in the Spanish-American emancipation against the Spanish empire. He said, "Slavery is the daughter of darkness. An ignorant people is a blind instrument of its own destruction."

This very apt phrase shows that the cause of slavery is ignorance, which also produces destruction. Now let's look at what the Word of God says:

"***My people are destroyed for lack of knowledge.*** *Because you have rejected knowledge, I also will reject you from being priest for Me; because you have forgotten the law of your God, I also will forget your children*" (Hosea 4:6 Author´s emphasis).

The lack of knowledge of God blinds people's eyes, reducing them to slavery, and therefore to the destruction of their lives. Lack of identity is the root of slavery. We have been freed and adopted as children of God through Christ:

"*For he who is called in the Lord while a slave is the Lord's freedman. Likewise he who is called while free is Christ's slave. You were bought at a price; do not become slaves of men*" (1 Corinthians 7:22-23).

The way to emancipate a slave was to pay the price of their freedom. This is exactly what Scripture says that Jesus Christ did for each one of us. In Him we are made free, that is, we´ve been given an identification card and all our rights have been restored. However, the lack of this knowledge wreaks havoc even among the people of God.

Having already spoken of physical slavery, I will now speak of spiritual slavery. You could be physically free but your soul could be imprisoned. Slavery ties your heart to pain, bitterness and reduces your soul to confinement. There are spiritual chains that don't allow you to dream. You feel alone and enslaved that you cannot move forward. Your vision disappears and you live feeling your way on the walls without knowing which way to go. In that context, these are the words of the psalmist:

"*Bring my soul out of prison, that I may praise Your name; the righteous shall surround me, For You shall deal bountifully with me*" (Psalm 142:7).

As is clear from this biblical passage, slavery has a central purpose and that is that you cannot praise God. For this reason, David asks the Lord to release him from his prison so he can praise Him, which means that as long as his soul was imprisoned it was impossible to praise. The history of the people of Israel illustrates this condition well. Let's read a fragment of what they lived under this system of slavery while Pharaoh ruled in the land of Egypt. Moses, whom the Lord chose to free the Israelites who were slaves, appeared before Pharaoh to ask him to let them go and celebrate a festival for God in the desert.

This was his response:

"*And Pharaoh said, ´Look, the people of the land are many now, and you make them rest from their labor!´ So the same day Pharaoh commanded the taskmasters of the people and their officers, saying, ´You shall no longer give the people straw to make brick as before. Let them go and gather straw for themselves. And you shall lay on them the quota of bricks which they made before. You shall not reduce it. For they are idle; therefore they cry out, saying, 'Let us go and sacrifice to our God.' Let more work be laid on the men, that they may labor in it, and let them not regard false words´*" (Exodus 5:5-9).

This passage shows me that Pharaoh, who represents the leader of the slavery government, will always add burdens to your life. Slavery seeks to keep you suffocating, busy, and tired. According to this Scripture, offering sacrifices to God means being idle, because only he who is from God understands the Word of God. But the one who is from the world does not understand the importance of loving the Father and spending time in His presence. Rest brings freedom, while weariness enslaves. How much of people's time do their jobs consume, even when they say everything they do is for their family? But a salary is not enough to pay the debt of absence. The consequences of slavery are devastating:

"*So the Egyptians made the children of Israel serve with rigor. And they made their lives bitter with hard bondage—in mortar, in brick, and in all manner of service in the field. All their service in which they made them serve was with rigor*" (Exodus 1:13-14).

If we were to describe Pharaoh in a single word it would be "oppressor."

An imprisoned soul originates from pain and trauma; from that which you've not been able to forgive. That feeling of resentment, hatred, even victimhood ends up making you more and more intolerant, bitter, and angry.

Pharaoh is not only a biblical character, he is also a spiritual agent, and Egypt is not just a country, but a system. The Word of God explains it like this:

"*And their dead bodies will lie in the street of the great city which spiritually is called Sodom and Egypt, where also our Lord was crucified*" (Revelation 11:8).

"*'The spirit of Egypt will fail in its midst; I will destroy their counsel, and they will consult the idols and the charmers, the mediums and the sorcerers. And the Egyptians I will give into the hand of a cruel master, and a fierce king will rule over them,' says the Lord, the Lord of hosts*" (Isaiah 19:3-4).

Many times in the face of pain and despair, people go to witches, sorcerers, and spiritual leaders of all kinds in hopes to get out of their anguish. Their ignorance becomes a transgression and confines the soul to this spiritual prison. God, whom David acknowledges, is the only One who can free you from this place of affliction. This spiritual practice referred to in Isaiah 19 brings bondage with it. The devil offers you freedom but the truth is that he himself is captive in this system that has confined him to eternal condemnation. The Word of God affirms it:

"Is this the man who made the earth tremble, who shook kingdoms, who made the world as a wilderness, who did not open the house of his prisoners?" (Isaiah 14:16b, 17b).

He never opened the jail for his prisoners because he didn't have the power to do so. Although these verses speak of the harshness and decadence of the king of Babylon, we know that Isaiah 14:1-17 also refers to Satan. The phrase, *"Who did not open the house of his prisoners"*, provides the truth that the only One who can free the soul is the heavenly Father.

"While they promise them liberty, they themselves are slaves of corruption; for by whom a person is overcome, by him also he is brought into bondage" (2 Peter 2:9).

Freedom comes the way God designed it, that is, only through Christ. But then, why are we in bondage? Because we don't know who we are and who our Father is. What is the relationship between slavery and fatherhood?

As we already know, God is the heavenly Father. The enemy constitutes a lie about who we are and who He is so that when you are in need, you go to the wrong source and therefore remain in slavery. Let's read this passage about what Jesus told the Jews who claimed to be children of Abraham:

"Then Jesus said to those Jews who believed Him, 'If you abide in My word, you are My disciples indeed'" (John 8:31).

In this passage, the word *if* is conditional, so let's analyze the benefits of abiding in Jesus:

"Abide in Me, and I in you. As the branch cannot bear fruit of itself, unless it abides in the vine, neither can you, unless you abide in Me. I am the vine, you are the branches. He who abides in Me, and I in him, bears much fruit; for without Me you can do nothing" (John 15:4-5).

Abiding in Jesus brings with it being grafted into the life of the Vine, which allows you to bear fruit. Abiding in Jesus will reveal the Father to you:

"All things have been delivered to Me by My Father, and no one knows the Son except the Father. Nor does anyone know the Father except the Son, and the one to whom the Son wills to reveal Him" (Matthew 11:27).

The revelation of the heavenly Father is only possible through Jesus, He is the only way to receive this great truth. An added benefit of abiding in Jesus is:

"If you abide in Me, and My words abide in you, you will ask what you desire, and it shall be done for you" (John 15:7).

Everyone who abides in Jesus will have what they long for, this is the Lord's promise in this passage. However, there's a purpose with the fruit of remaining:

"By this My Father is glorified, that you bear much fruit; so you will be My disciples" (John 15:8).

The purpose is to glorify the Father in everything, not to glorify ourselves. Orphanhood is to be separated from the Vine. Now, we all know that what makes the vine productive is the land in which it is planted. This is very true; Christ is the Vine. Let's read Who supports this statement:

"I am the true vine, and My Father is the vinedresser" (John 15:1).

Jesus is the channel through which the Father sends His nutrients. We understand that if we are separated from the Vine we lose the ability to know the Father, to bear fruit, and to glorify Him. We would be alone, isolated and we could not do anything.

Orphanhood is simply being separated from the Father. In the following Scripture there is a stark statement:

"If anyone does not abide in Me, he is cast out as a branch and is withered; and they gather them and throw them into the fire, and they are burned" (John 15:6).

This shows us what it feels like to be separated: it feels lonely, isolated, broken, and dry. A fire is produced, that day by day consumes the life within you until you completely lose the meaning of life. This is the reason why so many people have a great need of belonging and want to have all sorts of memberships; it's because they are separated from the source that sustains them. But everyone who abides in Jesus has the freedom to live in Him. What does slavery have to do with what we just read? Everything! We become slaves to the world when we consciously or unconsciously stay connected to the wrong source.

We´ve seen the importance of abiding in Jesus; the following verse explains the result of doing so:

"And you shall know the truth, and the truth shall make you free" (John 8:32).

What is truth? Christ is the truth. What does this truth reveal? The Father. Through the Spirit of the Son, we will be convinced that we are also children of God. The manifestation of the Spirit gives us Jesus´ capacity to have the identity of sons and daughters. It gives us the capacity to obey, to receive the revelation of the Father´s secrets, and to have and fulfill a destiny. And finally, the glory that comes with having done the will of the Father. This truth is so that we may bear much fruit and the Father may be glorified.

How many have felt slaves of another person, a circumstance, or a vice? Do we want to stop doing what destroys us but can't? Do we long to get away from that inconvenient relationship but it seems that our willpower is not enough? When many hear about slavery they think they´ve never been slaves, others relate it to the color of their skin. Slavery is physical, but also spiritual. The truth is that slavery is associated with lying, and Scripture certainly confirm this:

"'And you shall know the truth, and the truth shall make you free.' They answered Him, 'We are Abraham's descendants, and have never been in bondage to anyone. How can You say, 'You will be made free'?'" (John 8:32-33).

In this passage, Jesus is speaking with the Jews who had believed in Him. What truth was Jesus talking about? The one He came to reveal, as we saw in the chapter about worship. The fatherhood of God and abiding in Jesus brings with it the revelation that produces freedom. Now let's see how slavery is associated with being bound. The Jews took a certain position after what Jesus told them, let's read the verse again:

"They answered Him, 'We are Abraham's descendants, and have never been in bondage to anyone. How can You say, 'You will be made free'?'" (John 8:33).

Does being of the lineage of Abraham prevent you from being a slave? Does being from a wealthy, renowned family make you free? Maybe your father has a lot of purchasing power and a surname full of financial success; maybe he raised you or just gave you a life full of luxury, but do you feel free?

I had the opportunity to minister to a man about the fatherhood of God. To which he responded, "I come from an important family ancestry." However, at 40 years old, he had never heard of the gospel and was very attached to sexual sins such as adultery, orgies, and fornication. He had tainted his flesh as much as was possible because he was an angry and very rebellious man. Rebellious people taint their flesh. They´re slaves. However, this man considered himself "distinguished" because of the surname from which he came. He thought he was free. Let's read about the relationship Scripture makes between rebellion and the flesh:

"Likewise also these dreamers defile the flesh, reject authority, and speak evil of dignitaries" (Jude 1:8).

More on the subject:

"But these speak evil of whatever they do not know; and whatever they know naturally, like brute beasts, in these things they corrupt themselves" (Jude 1:10).

Finally: *"These are grumblers, complainers, walking according to their own lusts; and they mouth great swelling words, flattering people to gain advantage"* (Jude 1:16).

This man who considered himself a privileged son was simply a slave to sin, like the Jews who believed that their fatherhood was in Abraham and were "teachers" of a law that they didn't keep.

Let's look for the analogy in these Jews, who represent every one of us, because when we didn´t know the Word of God we believed we were not slaves.

These Jews were such wealthy and boastful orphans, but Jesus' statement includes a great revelation:

"Jesus answered them, ´Most assuredly, I say to you, whoever commits sin is a slave of sin. And a slave does not abide in the house forever, but a son abides forever´" (John 8:34-35).

According to the words of Jesus, sin enslaves you. You are not a slave because of your country, continent of origin, or your social condition; you are a slave because of sin. When a slave loses their strength or the interest of the one who had them bound is devalued, they are thrown out of the house and replaced. Have you ever felt like this? Did someone take advantage of you until you were no longer useful to them? Do you have any idea why you allow this type of abuse? This is one of the characteristics of slavery; you are rejected and you don´t stay in the house forever. Only those who have the revelation of God's fatherhood and experience it can remain in the Father's house.

Let's see the great connection between sexual sin and money in a fragment of the parable of the Prodigal Son:

"Then He said: ´A certain man had two sons. And the younger of them said to his father, 'Father, give me the portion of goods that falls to me.' So he divided to them his livelihood. And not many days after, the younger son gathered all together, journeyed to a far country, and there wasted his possessions with prodigal living. But when he had spent all, there arose a severe famine in that land, and he began to be in want. Then he went and joined himself to a citizen of that country, and he sent him into his fields to feed swine. And he would gladly have filled his stomach with the pods that the swine ate, and no one gave him anything´" (Luke 15:11-16).

I would say that this son in the parable is like the 40-year-old man I mentioned who said he was "of ancestry". Although he lacks identity because of his orphanhood, materially speaking, he had a father who could give him an inheritance. Even so, he chose to be a slave to sin and lost everything he had. Due to his lack of identity, his inheritance led him to prostitutes and a life full of ruin. If we could ask the Prodigal Son, before he received the inheritance, if he felt like an orphan or slave, he would´ve possibly answered no. But if we asked him the same question while he was taking care of the pigs, wanting to fill his belly with the carob beans the pigs ate, he would surely answer yes! Now he had to work to be able to eat and that made him a slave. He went from being a son to being a slave. So, if the Word of God says that the children remain in the house of the Father forever and the slave does not, we understand that he was never a son, he lived as an orphan!

In the words of the proverbist Solomon:

"Whoever loves wisdom makes his father rejoice, but a companion of harlots wastes his wealth" (Proverbs 29:3).

The Master continues by telling the "children of Abraham", *"The truth will set you free."* What truth does He speak of and free from what? The truth that you are a child of God, and made free from the sin that has bound you because you did not know the Father. In this sense, this freedom is from orphanhood.

"Therefore if the Son makes you free, you shall be free indeed" (Juan 8:36).

What does this truth mean? Who is Jesus talking about when He refers to the Son? To Himself, since all of the Father's authority was given to Christ to set you free. He not only speaks the truth, He *is* the truth. Freedom comes through knowing Jesus and being brought to the heavenly Father through Him. In this passage it's all about fatherhood:

"I know that you are Abraham's descendants, but you seek to kill Me, because My word has no place in you" (John 8:37).

Many people pursue the truth and claim to be free. Yet, they go against God because they do not accept His words and that Jesus is sent by the Father. To them, their father is Abraham, which means they do not have the revelation:

"I speak what I have seen with My Father, and you do what you have seen with your father" (John 8:38).

What Jesus claims here is because He was in the Father's presence. Notice that He talks about what He's seen, while the Jews only speak about what they've heard, that is, that Abraham is their father. Though this is what they heard and learned, they were still slaves. They insisted on their position, saying to Jesus:

"They answered and said to Him, ´Abraham is our father.´ Jesus said to them, ´If you were Abraham's children, you would do the works of Abraham´" (John 8:39).

Let´s recall that everyone who recognizes someone besides the heavenly Father as their father has a false identity, like the Samaritan Woman. But these Jews were even more wrong because they said they were children of Abraham without having faith. That's why Jesus said, *"If you were Abraham›s children, you would do the works of Abraham."* What works? Works of faith in God. See how Jesus confronts this supposed fatherhood in Abraham:

"But now you seek to kill Me, a Man who has told you the truth which I heard from God. Abraham did not do this" (John 8:40).

Do you know why they couldn't accept the truth? This Scripture has the answer:

"The Spirit of truth, whom the world cannot receive, because it neither sees Him nor knows Him; but you know Him, for He dwells with you and will be in you" (John 14:17).

The blindness about our beliefs is astonishing. Everything that is a lie will bind us. Even Abraham was not the father of these Jews; they rejected Jesus and the heavenly Father who sent Him:

"´You do the deeds of your father.´ Then they said to Him, ´We were not born of fornication; we have one Father—God´" (John 8:41).

These Jews called themselves children of God because they weren't children of fornication. They said this because they knew the law and, supported by their own prudence, believed that they could fulfill the law of God.

As Jesus confronted them, they went from declaring that they were children of Abraham to saying that they were children of God. Well, by now we see that they themselves did not know whose sons they were:

"Jesus said to them, ´If God were your Father, you would love Me, for I proceeded forth and came from God; nor have I come of Myself, but He sent Me. Why do you not understand My speech? Because you are not able to listen to My word´" (John 8:42-43).

We can comprehend why they didn't understand Jesus´ words. They certainly weren't of God, they were slaves; bound because of the lie about their father and themselves.

Really, they were neither children of Abraham nor children of God, they were just orphans. The following statement from Jesus is truly amazing:

"You are of your father the devil, and the desires of your father you want to do. He was a murderer from the beginning, and does not stand in the truth, because there is no truth in him. When he speaks a lie, he speaks from his own resources, for he is a liar and the father of it" (John 8:44).

In order for you to lose your identity, the devil needs to sow a lie. He displaces the biological father and consequently, the heavenly Father. When he does so, he positions himself as the father. This is the same thing that happened to the Prodigal Son. He didn't have the identity of a son with either father; his biological father who gave him the inheritance nor the heavenly Father, since he did

Satan´s works when he lived recklessly. The devil is a father. The heavenly Father sent Jesus so that through the *truth* we can have a relationship with Him as His sons and daughters; in the same way, through lies and false doctrines and beliefs, Satan seeks to keep people bound like his children. This is an imitation of true fatherhood. Notice how Jesus tells them that there is no truth in the enemy and that he is a liar. Because slavery is based on identity, we are enslaved when we don´t know the truth about who we are. We are not slaves not because of Abraham, but we are free because of Christ. He came to redeem us from the orphanhood we had due to our separation from the Father. I want to close this section with the following passage where Jesus tells them:

"Jesus answered, ´If I honor Myself, My honor is nothing. It is My Father who honors Me, of whom you say that He is your God´" (John 8:54).

With this statement, Jesus lets them see that the One the Jews called *God*, is His *Father*. How many people say, "I believe in God," but do not know Him as a Father and are orphaned. The first thing the enemy does to keep you in slavery is attack your identity. Then, he ties you down to painful memories that end up making you lose all your dignity. So you begin to put your confidence in material goods, people, academic achievements, social circles, even in positions of authority within the church. You do everything with the sole motivation of belonging.

Slavery is intrinsically linked to money. Let's read what Scripture says about this relationship:

"The rich rules over the poor, and the borrower is servant to the lender" (Proverbs 22:7).

He who has money becomes a lord. Money magnifies the one who has it and elevates them as ruler over those who don't. On the other hand, Scripture lets us see that debt takes us captive, even as slaves, to the one from whom you borrowed the loan. They become your master; a servitude is established in this relationship. What is a slave, a servant, entitled to? Nothing! There are spiritual chains that bind your life by falling into these ties. God's Word establishes it:

"For the love of money is a root of all kinds of evil, for which some have strayed from the faith in their greediness, and pierced themselves through with many sorrows" (1 Timothy 6:10).

Why is money loved? Because of lack of identity. This is the motivation behind greed. The pain that pierces through life is indescribable. This pain reduces you to a slave and strips you of your dignity as well as the ability to discern between the good and bad.

How many people would like to turn back time to the moment before they accepted that job, that business deal, that illicit relationship? Pain is at the end of this path. All of this happens because we don´t know who can really sustain us.

God's Word expresses it this way:

"No one can serve two masters; for either he will hate the one and love the other, or else he will be loyal to the one and despise the other. You cannot serve God and mammon" (Matthew 6:24).

"No servant can serve two masters; for either he will hate the one and love the other, or else he will be loyal to the one and despise the other. You cannot serve God and mammon" (Luke 16:13).

These two passages contain great revelation. As I shared previously, I was once a slave to this kind of bondage. I had so much debt that I didn't know how to get out of it, but as I dove deep in Scripture, the Father revealed to me the reason for this servitude that existed in my life. Let's read Elijah's statement to get the context. The people of Samaria were immersed in idolatry; some worshiped God and others Baal. And in this context, Elijah barged onto the scene:

"And Elijah came to all the people, and said, ´How long will you falter between two opinions? If the Lord is God, follow Him; but if Baal, follow him.´ But the people answered him not a word" (1 Kings 18:21).

We know that the Old Testament is a shadow and picture of what was to come. So Elijah´s statement is the same one Christ made when He taught about wealth. This is the only instance where the Lord is on the balance scale against another lord. To falter between two thoughts is to debate as to what lordship to accept over one's life.

The truth is that you will serve the one you acknowledge. God's people have been torn between these two thoughts due to their lack of identity as sons and daughters. Regarding this matter, Apostle Paul said:

"Now if their fall is riches for the world, and their failure riches for the Gentiles, how much more their fullness!" (Romans 11:12).

Obviously, this passage speaks of the remnant of the people of God. But let me ask you, what was Israel's transgression? Rejecting Christ. And since there are only two masters, the moment they rejected Christ they prostrated themselves before Baal. The deception is to accept being slaves. The enemy promises much more than what he can give you. The anxiousness to be acknowledged keeps you from resting in the Father's government:

"Now he who received seed among the thorns is he who hears the word, and the cares of this world and the deceitfulness of riches choke the word, and he becomes unfruitful" (Matthew 13:22).

"And the cares of this world, the deceitfulness of riches, and the desires for other things entering in choke the word, and it becomes unfruitful" (Mark 4:19).

It is evident that wealth is deceptive; it promises you freedom, but instead, you become its servant. Now, what is Baal looking for? Worship! That you remain prostrate before him:

"Again, the devil took Him up on an exceedingly high mountain, and showed Him all the kingdoms of the world and their glory. And he said to Him, 'All these things I will give You if You will fall down and worship me'" (Matthew 4:8-9).

Notice that among all the temptations Satan presented to Jesus in the wilderness, this is the one that had to do with wealth. What does the enemy ask of Him in exchange for giving Him the kingdoms and their glory? Worship!

The analogy with Paul's words in Romans 11:4 is surprising. Elijah cried out to God, feeling that he had been left alone to fight against the worshippers of Baal. The Lord responded:

"But what does the divine response say to him? 'I have reserved for Myself seven thousand men who have not bowed the knee to Baal'" (Romans 4:11).

Satan is Baal himself and what he wants is for you to bow down to him, become his servant and enslave your life. Don't accept to kneel before Baal, this is nothing more than the deceit of wealth. It creates painful expectations that will never be fulfilled. Let's read how Christ responded to the enemy's proposal about giving Him wealth:

"Then Jesus said to him, 'Away with you, Satan! For it is written, 'You shall worship the Lord your God, and Him only you shall serve''" (Matthew 4:10).

In Jesus' response, we see the relationship between worship and serving. If you worship the devil you will serve him, you will become his slave; if you prostrate yourself before him you will be taken captive. Jesus knew that He was the Son of God. In the same way, if you´re a son or daughter all that the Father has is yours:

"Therefore you are no longer a slave but a son, and if a son, then an heir of God through Christ" (Galatians 4:7).

You don't have to sell your freedom in exchange for sustenance, you have a Father who has made you the heir of all His riches, by grace. It isn't necessary for you to bow down to anything or anyone.

This promise that the heavenly Father made to Jesus Christ is the same one that He currently makes to all of His children, without any exception:

"I will declare the decree: The Lord has said to Me, 'You are My Son, today I have begotten You. Ask of Me, and I will give You the nations for Your inheritance, and the ends of the earth for Your possession" (Psalms 2:7-8).

As you can see, if you are a son or daughter, you are an heir. Even, an heir of the nations and to the ends of the earth. This promise is not for orphans, but for those He has begotten as children. Only sons and daughters are eligible to receive the inheritance.

Don't become a slave to something that rightfully **belongs to you!**

Sin makes you a slave, let's see:

"Do you not know that to whom you present yourselves slaves to obey, you are that one's slaves whom you obey, whether of sin leading to death, or of obedience leading to righteousness? But God be thanked that though you were slaves of sin, yet you obeyed from the heart that form of doctrine to which you were delivered. And having been set free from sin, you became slaves of righteousness. I speak in human terms because of the weakness of your flesh. For just as you presented your members as slaves of uncleanness, and of lawlessness leading to more lawlessness, so now present your members as slaves of righteousness for holiness. For when you were slaves of sin, you were free in regard to righteousness. What fruit did you have then in the things of which you are now ashamed? For the end of those things is death. But now having been set free from sin, and having become slaves of God, you have your fruit to holiness, and the end, everlasting life. For the wages of sin is death, but the gift of God is eternal life in Christ Jesus our Lord" (Romans 6:16-23).

Do you remember how we started this chapter? Talking about the Jews who claimed to be children of Abraham, to whom Jesus told them they were not children of Abraham but of the devil. What tied these people down? Lack of identity and the law:

"There is neither Jew nor Greek, there is neither slave nor free, there is neither male nor female; for you are all one in Christ Jesus. And if you are Christ's, then you are Abraham's seed, and heirs according to the promise" (Galatians 3:28-29).

The promise God made to Abraham that He would bless him is only received through faith:

"So then those who are of faith are blessed with believing Abraham" (Galatians 3:9).

If the Jews really knew who God was and the promise He had made to Abraham, they would´ve been blessed along with him. But instead, they were slaves to the law. This inheritance is conditional on maturity:

"Now I say that the heir, as long as he is a child, does not differ at all from a slave, though he is master of all, but is under guardians and stewards until the time appointed by the father. Even so we, when we were children, were in bondage under the elements of the world. But when the fullness of the time had come, God sent forth His Son, born of a woman, born under the law, to redeem those who were under the law, that we might receive the adoption as sons. And because you are sons, God has sent forth the Spirit of His Son into your hearts, crying out, ´Abba, Father!´ Therefore you are no longer a slave but a son, and if a son, then an heir of God through Christ" (Galatians 4:1-7).

How beautiful is the Word of God! We were slaves, but the heavenly Father adopted us through Christ. He removed the traps that bound us and the separation that existed between Him and us. He not only redeemed us from the law but also sent the Spirit of His Son. The Son gives us the conviction that through Him we are children of God, and if children, also heirs of all that the Father possesses. You can cry out when you need something, you do not have to prostrate yourself before Baal. The Father has adopted you to cry out to Him. Even if you never met your biological father, the heavenly Father has legally adopted you. It is a legal transaction through a payment, the blood of Jesus. And if you are adopted, you know that the most beautiful thing of all is that you weren't begotten by the father who raised you; but among so many children who didn't have parents, you were chosen.

This is even greater than being begotten, that someone who was able to choose another, gave their inheritance to you and freed you from slavery. The Lord's words in this passage confirm it:

"No longer do I call you servants, for a servant does not know what his master is doing; but I have called you friends, for all things that I heard from My Father I have made known to you. You did not choose Me, but I chose you and appointed you that you should go and bear fruit, and that your fruit should remain, that whatever you ask the Father in My name He may give you" (John 15:15-16).

In this sense, we´re all adopted, the Lord has chosen us above all else. This adoption is for the purpose of bearing fruit for His glory, for the secrets of the Father to be revealed to us through Jesus Christ, and so that we receive what we ask of Him.

Slavery is also associated with food and clothing. Slaves basically work for food. They are given a ration for each day's shift.

When you're an orphan, you´re a slave; you have no right to anything. One of the harsh experiences that accompanies this oppression is hunger fatigue. You must eat only what the masters want to give you, just like those who are confined in a prison only eat a small portion. The delicacies are reserved only for those who are free, for the sons and daughters. Those who´ve grown up in a boarding school, an orphanage, or simply been in spiritual slavery know that being full is very rare. Carrying a lordship other than that of Christ over your life will reduce you to slavery. There is always a lord; we are all subject to something or someone, whether to death in the case of sin or to justification in the case of the Lord Jesus.

Sons and daughters have the right to eat. I don´t know if perhaps you were the child of the woman who cleaned the house or of the gardener who took care of the flowers for a family. Maybe you sat at a distance and watched how the children of that family enjoyed their food while you were hungry. Though they offered you some, you didn't accept because you felt ashamed and embarrassed, even though you wanted to say yes. The food that was there was not for you, but for the house owner´s children. You saw them leave food on their plate or pick from everything they had. All you wanted to eat was what they threw out. The same happened to the Prodigal Son; *he wanted to fill his belly with the carob beans that the pigs ate, but nobody gave him any.* Could it be that God is unfair to give privileges to some and not to others? Maybe you›ve felt like that popular saying goes, like "no one›s son". Look at what the Scripture says:

"Therefore I say to you, do not worry about your life, what you will eat or what you will drink; nor about your body, what

you will put on. Is not life more than food and the body more than clothing? Look at the birds of the air, for they neither sow nor reap nor gather into barns; yet your heavenly Father feeds them. Are you not of more value than they?" (Matthew 6:25-26).

You are not "no one's child", you are the child of the Most High God through Jesus Christ. Your Father wants to feed you until you are satisfied and glorify His name. The reason there is hunger is that there is slavery and a lack of identity. In the Word of God, we find the cases of many who, while remaining in slavery or locked up in prisons, had a portion for each day, just like the current regime of a jail, orphanage, boarding school or spiritual prison.

Let's look at this verse:

"She also rises while it is yet night, and provides food for her household, and a portion for her maidservants" (Proverbs 31:15).

This passage is in the context of the virtuous woman God describes, highlighting her virtues. It says she feeds her family generously, but when speaking of her *maidservants*, the term used is *portion.* In my walk with God, I've met many people with childhoods marked by hunger. In the testimony chapter, I will tell you about a shocking case on this topic. Hunger makes you believe that you are worthless, that no one is there for you. When you're a kid and there's nothing to eat in your house you live sad, anguished, and you become selfish, not because you´re bad, but because when you have a little, you treasure it for fear of losing it. I want you to know that if this is your story, you have a Father who wants to sustain your life because you are worth much more than the birds of the sky, just cry out to Him.

This is a beautiful promise that God has left us in His Word:

"For the Lord your God is bringing you into a good land, a land of brooks of water, of fountains and springs, that flow out of valleys and hills; a land of wheat and barley, of vines and fig trees and pomegranates, a land of olive oil and honey; a land in which you will eat bread without scarcity, in which you will lack nothing; a land whose stones are iron and out of whose hills you can dig copper. When you have eaten and are full, then you shall bless the Lord your God for the good land which He has given you" (Deuteronomy 8:7-10).

Clothing is also included in the passage from Matthew 6:25-26 that you already read. The apostle Matthew, inspired by the Holy Spirit when he wrote this passage, displayed people's concern, who had anxiety in their hearts because of clothing. Slavery brings with it old, worn, cursed clothes. Many times, when you see a person, just by observing their way of dressing you can tell if they have a privileged position or not. In fact, royalty, priests, military, pilots, and medical personnel, among others, wear special clothing. When I look at the people who ask for money on the streets, I feel sadness and shame, because many times they are dirty and feel unworthy. How much trauma is produced for not having a dad to buy you your school uniform or graduation gown? There are wounds in the heart because of orphanhood in this area.

Let's look at some cases in which clothing had to do with being enslaved and also being imprisoned. Joseph was one of Jacob's 12 sons. His brothers sold him as a slave and he went through a process that lasted 13 years. In the last part of this process, Joseph was less than a slave, he was locked up in jail. You can imagine the clothes that were used in that place and the state of a person in that condition:

"Then Pharaoh sent and called Joseph, and they brought him quickly out of the dungeon; and he shaved, changed his clothing, and came to Pharaoh" (Genesis 41:14).

When he was taken out of that place, they changed his clothing. The changing of this garment has a physical, as well as a spiritual, significance. It represents the destruction of the curse. Can clothes represent a curse? Scripture states:

"As he clothed himself with cursing as with his garment" (Psalm 109:18a).

The revelation the Word of God brings to our lives is impressive. Let's read about another case:

"So Jehoiachin changed from his prison garments, and he ate bread regularly before the king all the days of his life" (Jeremiah 52:33).

To put you in context, this passage is about Jehoiachin, who was king of Judah. He was captive in a prison and when he was released, the same thing that happened to Joseph happened to him. They changed his clothes and he started eating like a king at his table. The subject of clothing is very interesting because the heavenly Father wants to dress you in the very best.

Let's read this beautiful promise:

"Her gain and her pay will be set apart for the Lord; it will not be treasured nor laid up, for her gain will be for those who dwell before the Lord, to eat sufficiently, and for fine clothing" (Isaiah 23:18).

The following passages further emphasize the close relationship between food and clothing, as Matthew also displays the Father's care:

"And yet I say to you that even Solomon in all his glory was not arrayed like one of these" (Matthew 6:29).

"Therefore do not worry, saying, 'What shall we eat?' or 'What shall we drink?' or 'What shall we wear?' For after all these things the Gentiles seek. For your heavenly Father knows that you need all these things. But seek first the kingdom of God and His righteousness, and all these things shall be added to you" (Matthew 6:31-33).

In these verses we find a pearl of great value, *"Seek first the kingdom of God and His righteousness, and all these things will be added to you."* This passage speaks of what we´ve been doing wrong in the face of our need when we ignore the Father. We´ve been looking for the things that are to be added to us, like food and clothing. It›s understandable that I act like this, because how do I look for His kingdom if I don›t even know that it exists? How do I cry out to the Father if my dad never took care of me? Well now you know, He takes care of you! Seek His kingdom and His righteousness will be established in your life. You will receive all of these add-ons and the Father will bring to life the promises that are in His Word for you. You are the heir to all of the Father´s riches. You are free to dream and create.

Prayer to receive God's Fatherhood and Freedom

(Slavery)

Heavenly Father, I present myself before You confessing that I have prostrated myself before false gods. I have sinned against You, leaving You for Baal, please forgive me. I recognize that my soul has been held captive in a prison because of it. Father only You, through Jesus Christ, can release my soul from this prison. Forgive me for faltering between two opinions and for looking for what I want instead of seeking your Kingdom and Your righteousness.

Free me from slavery, free me from poverty, free me from the demonic force of the oppressor. As You delivered the people of Israel out of Pharaoh's hand, set me free as well through Christ.

I renounce the spirit of Baal, I renounce slavery, I renounce idolatry, I renounce sorcery and I renounce poverty. I renounce the spirit of Egypt and I renounce the spirit of divination. I break every demonic pact that my ancestors, or I, have made. I break all pact with witchcraft and the occult. I plead the blood of Christ that made eternal redemption from all sin and ungodly covenants. Exchange my garments of curse for robes of righteousness and cover me with Your holiness. Father, I ask You to grant me the inheritance that corresponds to me as a child. Satisfy me with the necessary food, provide me with clothes and shelter.

I thank You for Your forgiveness, which I receive today through faith in Jesus Christ. Thank You because You have set me free through Your beloved Son. Father, I believe in Your promise to sustain me and I believe that I will also leave an inheritance to my children and my grandchildren.

Amen.

Chapter 6

Fatherhood and Power
(Intimidation)

Intimidation is a spiritual force linked to fear, terror, and fright, which seeks to stop the work of God. The intention behind this manifestation is subjection. Many children learn to live under this force because of how their parents raised them, others because they were blackmailed to receive sustenance (orphans or homeless folks). However, it's not voluntary obedience; the expectation of terror causes a coercive subjection, thus suppressing the person´s will. In many cases, intimidation poses a threat to a person's physical, mental, or emotional integrity.

From the knowledge of the Scriptures, I´d say that intimidation is generational. This means that the one who's been the victim of this controlling force becomes the one who exercises it over another. And so, the pattern continues. This is the reason for the battle over power: "He who has power controls," and the one who is subjected hopes to have the power to subdue others.

This practice can be learned by imitation or inherited patterns. Intimidation becomes so powerful over the human being that when the child becomes an adult, they feel vulnerable to it and fall into this subjection again. People in authority notice their weakness to defend their own will and they become that person´s slave. This force seeks to completely nullify any manifestation of power other than intimidation, going as far as killing in the struggle to dominate and achieve submission. The most emblematic case for the world is Adolf Hitler and his outrageous genocide against God's chosen people, the Jews! It's clear that behind intimidation there´s insecurity, an inferiority complex, and frustration of having been a victim of authority abuse, as well as a deep thirst for revenge and self-vindication. The Word of God says this about intimidation:

"My heart wavered, fearfulness frightened me; the night for which I longed He turned into fear for me" (Isaiah 21:4).

In the verse above, Isaiah expresses what he felt when God gave him the prophecy of the fall of Babylon. The words of the servant of God perfectly define what intimidation produces: paralysis and horror, as well as turning what he longed for into fear. Let's look at a few biblical examples of how intimidation works.

Ahab was the king of Israel in Samaria. The Assyrians had a king named Ben-hadad. This king gathered his entire army and brought with him 32 kings from other towns with horses and chariots. This enemy, because of the greatness of its army and its resources, was reputed to have fought and conquered others, so he tried to do the same with Samaria. Said king sent a threat through a messenger to the king of Israel, saying:

"Your silver and your gold are mine; your loveliest wives and children are mine" (1 Kings 20:3).

There are several facts we find in this message: the intention to intimidate, deprive, and dominate. If you let yourself be intimidated, they will rob you, and if you are robbed, you will be dominated. Now, this is King Ahab's answer:

"And the king of Israel answered and said, ´My lord, O king, just as you say, I and all that I have are yours´" (1 Kings 20:4).

Clearly, the fruit of intimidation took its toll on King Ahab. Not only did he declare that as king he submitted to Ben-hadad's lordship and authority, but he also accepted, without any opposition, the dispossession of all his property and the capture of his children and his wives. What would you think if you were this king´s wife or one of his sons? This is what happens when someone in authority tries to lead a family or a government without having a clear identity. Ahab wasn´t just anyone, he was the highest authority in Israel, yet it seems that he didn't even know it. The Assyrian king's reaction was to reiterate the intimidating threat:

"Then the messengers came back and said, ´Thus speaks Ben-Hadad, saying, 'Indeed I have sent to you, saying, ´You shall deliver to me your silver and your gold, your wives and your children´; but I will send my servants to you tomorrow about this time, and they shall search your house and the houses of your servants. And it shall be, that whatever is pleasant in your eyes, they will put it in their hands and take it'" (1 Kings 20:5-6).

Intimidation begins with a threat, but it never gets enough. Once the intimidator understands that the victim has submitted, they begin to tighten their reins until they leave the other person with nothing. The Assyrian king asked for Ahab´s property and family, Ahab gave him authority and even his own life when he said, "I am yours." However, all of this was not enough. The Assyrian king then asked for the most valuable thing from Ahab and his servants, to enter their houses to search and plunder them. What was King Ahab's response to this demand? Let's see:

"So the king of Israel called all the elders of the land, and said, ´Notice, please, and see how this man seeks trouble, for he sent to me for my wives, my children, my silver, and my gold; and I did not deny him´" (1 Kings 20:7).

The king of Israel consulted the elders of the country not out of wisdom, but out of fear. He had already given a declaration submitting to the authority of the Assyrian king before seeking their counsel. Ahab acted like the child who looks for his older brother to defend him at school. The reason is that Ahab didn´t have the revelation of God's power and had been intimidated by the Assyrians´ fame. What was the response of the elders of Israel?

"And all the elders and all the people said to him, ´Do not listen or consent´" (1 Kings 20:8).

The elders declared this answer because they knew the power of God. Now the king, backed by the elders and the people, with a newfound courage, sends his reply:

"Therefore he said to the messengers of Ben-Hadad, ´Tell my lord the king, 'All that you sent for to your servant the first time I will do, but this thing I cannot do.'´ And the messengers departed and brought back word to him" (1 Kings 20:9).

King Ahab's response is incredible. Note that these ambassadors spoke on behalf of the Assyrian king, while the king of Israel had to personally give answers to the servants. This is one of the strategies of the intimidators, to send messengers.

Ahab is not being sincere with the advice that the elders gave him. His lack of identity is so great that he places himself in the position of a servant to the Assyrian king; he still did not have the courage to simply say, "I am not going to obey you." Rather, he claims he will comply with the first demand of the Assyrian king, to which Ben-hadad replied:

"Then Ben-Hadad sent to him and said, ´The gods do so to me, and more also, if enough dust is left of Samaria for

a handful for each of the people who follow me´" (1 Kings 20:9-10).

It's impressive how the intimidator increases the threat. He not only has armies, chariots, and horses but now boasts that he has spiritual forces on his behalf and his followers. Undoubtedly, intimidation will use this type of sorcery to bend the person´s will using terror and fright, therefore paralyzing every possible form of defense. You can't negotiate with intimidation. From the very first message, it's necessary to declare absolute opposition. However, this time, the response of the king of Israel is accompanied by divine inspiration:

"So the king of Israel answered and said, ´Tell him, 'Let not the one who puts on his armor boast like the one who takes it off'´" (1 Kings 20:11).

This is a declaration of setting himself free. Now King Ahab is making use of his authority. He tells the Assyrian king that the manifestation of God's power is not in the armor they wear. What will bring victory to God's people is the power of God's Spirit, as the prophet says:

"Suddenly a prophet approached Ahab king of Israel, saying, ´Thus says the Lord: 'Have you seen all this great multitude? Behold, I will deliver it into your hand today, and you shall know that I am the Lord'´" (1 Kings 20:13).

With the prophet´s words and the following passage, I can conclude this:

"So he answered and said to me: ´This is the word of the Lord to Zerubbabel: 'Not by might nor by power, but by My Spirit,' Says the Lord of hosts´" (Zechariah 4:6).

What paralyzes intimidation is the manifestation of the power of God's Spirit over a life, a people, or a kingdom. Everything is subject to the authority of the armies of the living God. And there are more stories like this one: Elijah and Jezebel, Hezekiah and Sennacherib, David and Goliath. All of their stories include intimidation, their adversaries´ boasting, the sending of messengers, threats, and the self-proclaimed victory from the demonic forces. The intention is the same: to intimidate, steal, and dominate.

Not every case was like King Ahab's story. For example, David wasn't king at the time, he was a simple shepherd boy in his adolescent years. But he didn't even flinch before the threats of Goliath, the giant Philistine, because his identity was anchored in what he knew he could do through the power of God. On the contrary, he was outraged at the absurd threats made by an uncircumcised man, by one who was not in covenant with God.

In every single case, intimidation begins with words which is undoubtedly an imitation of the flow of faith:

"So then faith comes by hearing, and hearing by the word of God" (Romans 10:17).

In this same way, the enemy uses hearing to frighten and try to stop the construction of God's work. Just like Nehemiah´s adversaries, Tobias, Sanballat, and Geshem, did with him according to Nehemiah 6:1-19.

Consider the relationship intimidation has to orphanhood and fatherhood to power.

The lack of identity tolerates intimidation which is in the same family as fear, as we saw in the chapter on love. Another level of this is terror or fright. Many people, even knowing Jesus Christ, are victims of the threat posed by authorities since they compromise the truth because of reprisals. Both the bully and the bullied have an identity problem. Jesus Christ is our teacher in everything, and through the passage we studied in the first book of Kings, we learned that intimidation is defeated with the power of the Spirit of God.

Jesus Christ came to earth as a man. When He was baptized, the Holy Spirit came upon Him. And after being in the wilderness, He began His ministry with power. He exercised this power by preaching the good news, healing the sick, opening the eyes of the blind, and casting out demons. He did all of this with the power of God. At the time, traditional religion held the religious monopoly, so it was very threatening to them that Jesus performed these miracles. They knew the law, but as we saw in the chapter on grace, Jesus embodied the favor of God, forgiving sins and undoing the works of the devil. They claimed Jesus was a blasphemer and that He should die because of it. In the religious sphere, the one trying to intimidate always seeks to discredit the source of power. The Pharisees said that Jesus performed miracles in the name of Beelzebul. However, Jesus answered that the devil could not be the one doing those works because it was impossible for him to cast out his own kingdom. It was simply the works of Jesus that supported the assignment the Father had given

Him. It came from Him, through His power. Before the death of Lazarus, the Jews said:

"And some of them said, 'Could not this Man, who opened the eyes of the blind, also have kept this man from dying? '" (John 11:37).

Of course, they weren't interested in Lazarus, they only murmured to discredit Jesus. But the manifestation of power they were about to witness would leave them speechless since Lazarus had been dead for four days:

"Then they took away the stone from the place where the dead man was lying. And Jesus lifted up His eyes and said, 'Father, I thank You that You have heard Me. And I know that You always hear Me, but because of the people who are standing by I said this, that they may believe that You sent Me.' Now when He had said these things, He cried with a loud voice, 'Lazarus, come forth!'" (John 11:41-43).

This is the power of God in the flesh. In a case like this one, there are no arguments or discrediting matters that can obscure the evidence. The Holy Spirit is the only One who can give life and Jesus credited His Father with this wonder. But what was the Pharisees' position?

"Then the chief priests and the Pharisees gathered a council and said, 'What shall we do? For this Man works many signs. If we let Him alone like this, everyone will believe in Him, and the Romans will come and take away both our place and nation'" (John 11:47-48).

The Pharisees had poison on their tongues and used lies as a weapon of manipulation. It wasn´t true that the Romans would destroy their holy place and nation; their concern was that the people would begin to believe in Jesus because of the miracles He did. They didn't care about Lazarus´ life. Inspired by the prophecy, they themselves said what the purpose of Jesus' death was. It inconvenient for them for Jesus to die for the nation:

"And not for that nation only, but also that He would gather together in one the children of God who were scattered abroad. Then, from that day on, they plotted to put Him to death" (John 11:52-53).

The truth is that the death of Jesus reconciled us with the fatherhood of God so that the works that He did, we can also do. However, for this, we need to be gathered with the Father through Jesus, as the verse we just read says. Jesus was an instrument of God's power and He paid the price of being persecuted by these Pharisees. Let's read what happened to some of the Jews who saw the resurrection of Lazarus:

"But the chief priests plotted to put Lazarus to death also, because on account of him many of the Jews went away and believed in Jesus" (John 12:10-11).

This passage shows that they not only wanted to kill Jesus but also the one who witnessed His power, Lazarus! It was all because they were losing the hold they had over the people. This is something that continues today in a similar way. There are some religious leaders, pastors, and priests who want to obscure the powerful works of some of Jesus´ disciples because they simply cannot do them because of their own lack of identity and insecurity. It is for this reason that they choose to try to hide others´ gifts and miracles to prevent exactly the following from happening:

"The Pharisees therefore said among themselves, ´You see that you are accomplishing nothing. Look, the world has gone after Him!´" (John 12:19).

It's very ironic, but it's because of the dominion that Satan has over the world; he thinks he's the owner. However, Jesus came as the Savior of the world. For this reason, it's evident that people went after Him; people need help and freedom. That is why they don't want to hear more words, what they need is the manifestation of God's power. That's really what can change people's lives. However, for many religious leaders, power has become a threat. How far can intimidation go? Let's read:

"Nevertheless even among the rulers many believed in Him, but because of the Pharisees they did not confess Him, lest they should be put out of the synagogue" (John 12:42).

This is intimidation, the fear of retaliation. Does the same happen in today's society? Of course, and not just among God's people. Does this happen in governments? In small groups? Between blood brothers? Between different religions? Is this a form of communism? Yes, it's a strategy to control the mind. Feeling intimidated because of the fear of being expelled from the group or the church. What is the reason for selling the truth and compromising faith in God? The following verse has the answer:

"For they loved the praise of men more than the praise of God" (John 12:43).

Simply put, they do not have the identity of sons and daughters. Jesus was Son and everything the Father sent Him to say, He said. Now, if the Father has sent you to say something, why don't you say it? What was the difference with Jesus? Did Jesus say what He wanted or was He led by the Father?

"For I have not spoken on My own authority; but the Father who sent Me gave Me a command, what I should say and what I should speak. And I know that His command is everlasting life. Therefore, whatever I speak, just as the Father has told Me, so I speak" (John 12:49-50).

So, if the Father has not spoken to you, logically you do not have the revelation of His power and fatherhood in your life, since the Word of God establishes:

"For as many as are led by the Spirit of God, these are sons of God" (Romans 8:14).

If you don't know what to do and do not recognize the guidance of the Spirit of God, you have not received the adoption established by this passage:

"For you did not receive the spirit of bondage again to fear, but you received the Spirit of adoption by whom we cry out, 'Abba, Father'" (Romans 8:15).

This is the seal in our spirit that bears witness to our identity as children of God and leads us to do the will of the Father, even above our own. Without the spirit of adoption, we are orphans and live in fear. The manifestation of Divine power is what characterizes a true child of God.

Jesus said:

"Do you not believe that I am in the Father, and the Father in Me? The words that I speak to you I do not speak on My own authority; but the Father who dwells in Me does the works. Believe Me that I am in the Father and the Father in Me, or else believe Me for the sake of the works themselves" (John 14:10-11).

Do you have God's fatherhood? Do you live it out? If so, then you can believe in the manifestation of His power. If not, there is still orphanhood. Jesus reaffirms this:

"And I will pray to the Father, and He will give you another Helper, that He may abide with you forever" (John 14:16).

And He continues to say:

"I will not leave you orphans; I will come to you" (John 14:18).

This is the Father's promise. That through Jesus He will not leave us as orphans. That through His Spirit we will be guided as children to do the works that He did, to be free from intimidation, just like Jesus, and to do the will of our Father, despite death threats, criticism, murmuration, sectarianism, or retaliation.

What is the reason for these divisions and the Pharisees´ attitude?

"These things I have spoken to you, that you should not be made to stumble. They will put you out of the synagogues; yes, the time is coming that whoever kills you will think that he offers God service. And these things they will do to you because they have not known the Father nor Me" (John 16:1-3).

All of the reasoning that was hidden behind the Pharisees is impactful. For although they said they were children of Abraham, they were really only descendants according to the flesh but not children of the promise. In this, we know those who are of the faith because they can manifest the power of the Father. On the other hand, those who are of the flesh are orphans; they are descendants of Abraham, but children of the slave, that is, children of the law. All of the persecution and insecurity are a result of the fact that they do not know the Father but still believe that they´re God's servants.

Isn't this intimidation exercised by religion the same feeling the person who converts to Christ experiences even today? Society practically discards them as if sin were a reason to boast and Christ someone to be ashamed of, making faith in Jesus Christ worthy of contempt and shame.

Isn't this the same intimidation that those who are involved in witchcraft suffer when they are told that the dead will take revenge if they leave them? Isn't this the very intimidation that Muslims use to kill in the name of faith or to terrify the believers of Islam? Isn't this the same intimidation that other religions exert on their parishioners? Of course, it is.

The promise given to those who believe is that they will not be left as orphans. On the other hand, the one who has not received adoption is an orphan; orphanhood is their spiritual condition. But the evidence of adoption is power. Let's go back to Scripture. Pilate insisted that he found no crime of death against Jesus, but why were the Pharisees so enraged with Jesus? Why did He need to die?

"The Jews answered him, 'We have a law, and according to our law He ought to die, because He made Himself the Son of God'" (John 19:7).

The law persecuted the Son of God, orphanhood pursued the Son of God. This was the big argument they had: that Jesus Christ was the Son of God and they were not!

Then, they used the same intimidation strategy with Pilate again. Faced with his refusal to kill Jesus for not finding sin in Him, they threatened him:

"From then on Pilate sought to release Him, but the Jews cried out, saying, 'If you let this Man go, you are not Caesar's

friend. Whoever makes himself a king speaks against Caesar´" (John 19:12).

Why did Pilate give in to this intimidation? We already know, *"because they loved the glory of men more than the glory of God."* Orphanhood takes away your identity and will, and can lead you to the point of crucifying the truth.

Throughout Jesus' walk on earth, He referred to the heavenly Father as, "My Father" or "the Father." However, after He was crucified, reconciled us, removed our orphanhood, and before returning to the Father He said:

"Jesus said to her, ´Do not cling to Me, for I have not yet ascended to My Father; but go to My brethren and say to them, ´I am ascending to My Father and your Father, and to My God and your God'" (John 20:17).

This message was so important that Jesus could not ascend without teaching them reconciliation and, furthermore, that the fatherhood of Jesus was now ours. It is vital to understand the phrase, *"But go to My brothers, and tell them, ´I am ascending to My Father and your Father, and to My God and your God.'"* This was pronounced by the Lord after He suffered the wrath of God and the curse because of our sin and satisfied the Father›s demand with the shedding of His blood. At that moment the separation was mended, it disappeared forever; the Father and God of Christ became the Father and God of all of us who believe and receive Jesus. However, let›s see how Jesus› disciples lived before learning these truths about reconciliation, fatherhood, and power:

"Then, the same day at evening, being the first day of the week, when the doors were shut where the disciples were assembled, for fear of the Jews, Jesus came and stood in the midst, and said to them, 'Peace be with you.' When He had said this, He showed them His hands and His side. Then the disciples were glad when they saw the Lord. So Jesus said to them again, 'Peace to you! As the Father has sent Me, I also send you.' And when He had said this, He breathed on them, and said to them, 'Receive the Holy Spirit'" (John 20:19-22).

They were hiding for fear of the Jews; scared, intimidated, and behind closed doors like the one who has no power. The evidence of Jesus' resurrection is wonderful; to see His hands and His side. If you are afraid, you need to see Jesus' scars because this is when dread is finally broken. The disciples saw that the Father had kept His word; He raised up the Son and they were clothed with the power that had raised Him up. From that day on they were sent to do what Jesus did: heal and resurrect people. The reason there are so many powerless believers is that they are unaware of God's fatherhood! The child flows with the power of the Father, as Jesus did, and nothing and no one intimidates them. Finally, Jesus commanded His disciples not to leave Jerusalem because they would receive the Father's promise. Certainly, the power that they personally received from Jesus is not a blessing just for the chosen apostles, but for everyone who believes in Jesus Christ as their Lord and Savior.

"But you shall receive power when the Holy Spirit has come upon you; and you shall be witnesses to Me in Jeru-

salem, and in all Judea and Samaria, and to the end of the earth" (Acts 1:8).

This power is the Father's strength, the manifestation of His glory, the reason why His Spirit was sent to earth so that by receiving Him we can be His witnesses. It is impossible to be witnesses of the Father if we are in orphanhood. We must be witnesses of the Father as Jesus was during His ministry on earth. Every miracle was manifested so that the Father would be glorified in the Son. We must also glorify the Father through the fruit of our lives. Only through His power is it possible to be witnesses. It is impossible to witness something that we have not seen or heard. How did this promise come about?

"When the Day of Pentecost had fully come, they were all with one accord in one place. And suddenly there came a sound from heaven, as of a rushing mighty wind, and it filled the whole house where they were sitting. Then there appeared to them divided tongues, as of fire, and one sat upon each of them. And they were all filled with the Holy Spirit and began to speak with other tongues, as the Spirit gave them utterance" (Acts 2:1-4).

This is how this power flows. One day, while we were ministering at church, a woman arrived who had participated in a religion that uses the bones of the dead to make witchcraft. When we told her about Jesus Christ, she said that the dead were going to retaliate against her, as this was what they had taught her. She was a prisoner of fear and lived completely terrified, so we answered her with this Scripture:

"And besides all this, between us and you there is a great gulf fixed, so that those who want to pass from here to you cannot, nor can those from there pass to us" (Luke 16:26).

This parable about the rich man and Lazarus makes it very clear that the dead cannot leave where they are to torment anyone, and much less take revenge.

The woman began to cry and told us, "They´ve deceived me all this time." This is intimidation. She not only believed that the dead would avenge her if she left that religion, but that she did the works of witchcraft with the dead, something we´ve already seen is impossible. Clearly, these were not the dead, but demons.

On the day of her deliverance, she was not only free from all demonic oppression over her life, but the Holy Spirit came upon her as she began to glorify the Father in new tongues of worship. That is the power of God! Can this woman testify of God? Of course, she can, the apostle Paul said:

"For the kingdom of God is not in word but in power" (1 Corinthians 4:20).

"And my speech and my preaching were not with persuasive words of human wisdom, but in demonstration of the Spirit and of power" (1 Corinthians 2:4).

"For our gospel did not come to you in word only, but also in power, and in the Holy Spirit and in much assurance, as you know what kind of men we were among you for your sake" (1 Thessalonians 1:5).

A child of God must manifest the power of the Father to undo the works of the devil and for the Father to be glorified in us as His children. Each one of us manifests the Father and the Son, so we are not ashamed and no one can belittle us:

"For I am not ashamed of the gospel of Christ, for it is the power of God to salvation for everyone who believes, for the Jew first and also for the Greek" (Romans 1:16).

So dear brothers and sisters, we must not be intimidated by anything.

"And not in any way terrified by your adversaries, which is to them a proof of perdition, but to you of salvation, and that from God" (Philippians 1:28).

As children of God, we live under the power of His Spirit, manifesting wonders and signs in His name. Not at all intimidated. In conclusion, can you imagine what would happen if Jesus Christ, intimidated by the Jews, had not done the will of the Father? We would be separated from Him, lost, and orphans without any hope of glory. Jesus, our example in everything, teaches us to be brave. He helps us reach the destiny the Father designed for each of His children. Your reason for living is linked to another person's purpose.

"We know that whoever is born of God does not sin, but he who has been born of God keeps himself, and ***the wicked one does not touch him****"* (1 John 5:8 Author´s emphasis).

Prayer to receive God's Fatherhood and Power

(Intimidation)

Heavenly Father, I come before Your presence recognizing that I have harbored intimidation in my heart. Today I forgive everyone who exercised control over me, I forgive everyone who has manipulated, intimidated, controlled, dominated, and deprived me. I forgive my parents for their blackmail. I forgive any person who, having authority over me, abused me through beatings, mistreatment, humiliation, offenses, threats, or repression with inappropriate words.

I renounce intimidation, I renounce terror, I renounce fear. I renounce control, I renounce manipulation, I renounce the Jezebel spirit. I renounce any demonic force that wants to exert paralysis on me or stop the flow of your Holy Spirit in me. I renounce to impose my point of view, I renounce to exercise dominion, control, and manipulation in the lives of others.

I cry out for Your Holy Spirit, for Your Word says that I will receive power when Your Spirit has come upon me.

By faith, I believe that You fill me with Your power to resist Satan. I believe no one will be able to come against me because as You were with Moses, You will be with me to free me.

I thank You for Your promise poured out at Pentecost. Because I know it is also for this time, I will witness all that Your Spirit of power does through me and I will speak Your truths without fear. I thank You because when I share Your Word, signs, miracles, and wonders will accompany my message. I thank You because Your power is in me making me brave in every situation. Amen.

Chapter 7

Fatherhood and Glory

(Hypocrisy)

Hypocrisy means to be fake with oneself, with others, and with God. Hypocrisy is a mask we wear physically or spiritually. It is rooted in pretending since the person tries to be someone they´re not and hide their true personality. Hypocrisy is evident in the person who lacks identity. When they look to the mirror they reject themself. Because a person wishes to be someone else, they try to embody the role that best fits their desires and interprets the imaginary life that they´ve idealized.

Hypocrisy makes a person engage in broken and superficial relationships because it does not allow them to approach people honestly about who they are. False expectations are generated but never fulfilled since sooner or later one disappoints the other when they show a bit of their true personality. Therefore, the attraction is fractured and the other person in the relationship is frustrated. This means that the person cannot have long-lasting friends or relationships and, hardest of all, it is impossible for them to have a relationship with God. The reason for this ordeal is lack of identity and fear of rejection.

In Greek etymology, the word *hypocrisy* comes from the word *hypocrite*, which was represented by an actor. On the contrary, *honesty* or *sincerity*, refer to the person who lives out in the open. This is David's statement about integrity:

"*I have not sat with idolatrous mortals, nor will I go in with hypocrites*" (Psalm 26.4).

In the context of the office of a prophet, the Word of God refers to hypocrisy:

"*For the land is full of adulterers; for because of a curse the land mourns. The pleasant places of the wilderness are dried up. Their course of life is evil, and their might is not right*" (Jeremiah 23:10).

According to what we saw in the previous chapter, intimidation tries to stop the movement of God's power by causing fear. On this occasion, God is speaking against the prophets who watered down the Word that God commanded them to communicate because they lacked godly courage.

"*Also I have seen a horrible thing in the prophets of Jerusalem: they commit adultery and walk in lies; they also strengthen the hands of evildoers, so that no one turns back from his wickedness. All of them are like Sodom to Me, and her inhabitants like Gomorrah. 'Therefore thus says the Lord of hosts concerning the prophets: 'Behold, I will feed them with wormwood, and make them drink the water of gall; for from the prophets of Jerusalem profaneness has gone out into all the land'"* (Jeremiah 23:14-15).

In this passage in Jeremiah, the Lord makes a very strong rebuke for the insincerity of His messengers and later assures them that they´ve sweetened His words with flattery. God's prophets are His mouth on earth. We could say that they are carriers of the power of God. So why would a person who has been clothed by His power fall into folly, lies and flattery? Why would they water down the Word of God? God Himself says, *"For from the prophets of Jerusalem profaneness (hypocrisy) has gone out into all the land"*. This is one of the conquests of intimidation; it suppresses the courage that a messenger of God must have. When identity is not established as it should be, Satan uses the prophets as his own servants.

Look at the following expression: *"They also strengthen the hands of evildoers"*. Certainly the one who has been called as a prophet of God can strengthen others. However, in the absence of identity, they end up compromising God's Word and favoring those who do not live in righteousness.

From everything we've discussed, we know that the Pharisees did not have the identity of children of God. In Matthew 23, Jesus unmasks with great vehement the hypocrisy of the scribes and Pharisees. In this passage the personality of the hypocrite is reflected:

"Then Jesus spoke to the multitudes and to His disciples, saying: ´The scribes and the Pharisees sit in Moses' seat. Therefore whatever they tell you to observe, that observe and do, but do not do according to their works; for they say, and do not do´" (Matthew 23:1-3).

We begin with a warning from Jesus. Moses´ seat referred to the study of the law. Because there isn't anything corrupt in the law, Jesus teaches that everything should be kept and done as explained to them. However, He makes His first reference to hypocrisy, revealing that the Pharisees and writers taught what they themselves did not comply with.

"For they bind heavy burdens, hard to bear, and lay them on men's shoulders; but they themselves will not move them with one of their fingers" (Matthew 23:4).

The Pharisees burdened people with rituals, impositions, demands, and traditions, though they themselves did not want to carry them on their shoulders.

"But all their works they do to be seen by men. They make their phylacteries broad and enlarge the borders of their garments" (Matthew 23:5).

Everything the Pharisees did upheld their holiness in opposition to the rest of the people. They wore garments that reflected their spiritual condition. They hung phylacteries from their garments, which were little boxes, or small leather cases, that held fragments of Scripture on parchment paper.

"They love the best places at feasts, the best seats in the synagogues..." (Matthew 23:6)

For the Pharisees, recognition was of utmost importance. Sitting in the front rows distinguished them from the rest of the people, which was really the motivation in their hearts.

"Greetings in the marketplaces, and to be called by men, 'Rabbi, Rabbi'" (Matthew 23:7).

Again, we see that acknowledgement was like the air they breathed. Their greetings had to be distinctive and with the mention that they were teachers. Saying, *"Rabbi, Rabbi,"* was like calling out to them or what someone says to get the attention of the renowned person they follow.

"But you, do not be called 'Rabbi'; for One is your Teacher, the Christ, and you are all brethren" (Matthew 23:8).

Let's remember that Jesus was teaching ordinary people and His disciples, and *they* would be the ones to succeed Him when He left. So He tells them very clearly that they should not hold the title of Rabbi or Teacher because this position of honor was reserved only for Him. He expresses that the Son of God came to show the Kingdom and reveal the Truth. There was and is only one Master for that task and He was the One who was speaking with them. Others could teach what the Spirit of Truth taught them, but that would not make them Rabbis, Christs, or Teachers. It is not a peculiar revelation that Jesus makes here, since this title is persecuted by precursors of false doctrines, such as the Masons who call themselves "Venerable teachers." The Word of God says that *He personally gave some to be teachers*, as a call to the ministry. But these teachers should only teach what Christ came to reveal, that is, the teachings of the Teacher of teachers, not personal arguments or doctrines of men different from those revealed by Jesus. This teacher that Jesus Christ constituted is a representation of Him in that role.

"Do not call anyone on earth your father; for One is your Father, He who is in heaven" (Matthew 23:9).

Calling themselves fathers was another custom the Pharisees had. It was a very distinguished position that even Jesus did not take for Himself. Would this clarification seem like an incongruity with the father who begot them? So what should the earthly father be called? Jesus is not referring to a person´s earthly father, but to God´s fatherhood and to the spiritual authority that this relationship implies, since the first commandment with a promise given by God says:

"Honor your father and your mother, that your days may be long upon the land which the Lord your God is giving you" (Exodus 20:12).

The imperative form that Jesus uses before this declaration gives us an idea that at that time it was very common to call mentors and teachers, "father". It was perhaps understandable because the fatherhood of God had not yet been revealed by Jesus and the separation had not yet been mended through the cross. But from what we can see, we're living in a similar time. The words of Jesus have been ignored since today many have mistakenly called themselves "spiritual fathers".

"*And do not be called teachers; for One is your Teacher, the Christ*" (Matthew 23:10).

The first time, He encouraged them to not be called teachers. But this time, He commands them not to be called teachers, making it clear that it is a position for the Son of God, the Christ, referring to His spiritual condition as Messiah and Anointed One.

"*But he who is greatest among you shall be your servant*"(Matthew 23:11).

In this statement, He reveals the Pharisees´ intentions, which were to be greater, distinguished, and set apart. But Jesus tells them that if that was their intention, they needed to be servants. Thus revealing that things in heaven are much different than here on earth.

"*And whoever exalts himself will be humbled, and he who humbles himself will be exalted*" (Matthew 23:12).

This was what the Pharisees did; they exalted and boasted about themselves. But Jesus emphasized that the servant would be exalted and He knew this very well in His own life.

"But woe to you, scribes and Pharisees, hypocrites! For you shut up the kingdom of heaven against men; for you neither go in yourselves, nor do you allow those who are entering to go in" (Matthew 23:13).

On this occasion, He directs His teaching to the scribes and Pharisees. He tells them that their behavior has closed the door for others to know the kingdom; by not behaving in a pious and humble way, it was impossible for others to want to know God. They themselves did not enter the kingdom and the burden was so great that no one could access God.

"Woe to you, scribes and Pharisees, hypocrites! For you devour widows' houses, and for a pretense make long prayers. Therefore you will receive greater condemnation" (Matthew 23:14).

They devoured widows by manipulating them, obtaining money from them in exchange for their prayers. *Devour* is the same word the book of Malachi uses to identify the work of Satan when he tries against or steals the fruit of our labor.

This is why Jesus called them hypocrites and let them know that their condemnation would be greater than that of those who sinned without hypocrisy. After all, they knew the Holy Scriptures and knew that widows were protected by God in a special way.

"Woe to you, scribes and Pharisees, hypocrites! For you travel land and sea to win one proselyte, and when he is won,

you make him twice as much a son of hell as yourselves" (Matthew 23:15).

The word *proselyte* refers to the effort made by the scribes and Pharisees to get others to be circumcised and accept the Jewish laws. However, this task lacked the correct intention in the heart. It wasn't about leading people to God, it was focused on their benefit, which is why Jesus called them hypocrites. Additionally, once people converted to Judaism, they were tied to eternal condemnation, just as sects do to this day.

"Woe to you, blind guides, who say, 'Whoever swears by the temple, it is nothing; but whoever swears by the gold of the temple, he is obliged to perform it.' Fools and blind! For which is greater, the gold or the temple that sanctifies the gold?" (Matthew 23:16-17).

Those who followed them were as blind as they were. Such was the ignorance of the scribes and Pharisees; they despised the temple even though it was the place where the presence of God was manifested. But still they imposed their threat and debt as a burden against whoever depleted the gold in the temple.

"And, 'Whoever swears by the altar, it is nothing; but whoever swears by the gift that is on it, he is obliged to perform it.' Fools and blind! For which is greater, the gift or the altar that sanctifies the gift?" (Matthew 23:18-19).

Jesus answered them:

"Therefore he who swears by the altar, swears by it and by all things on it. He who swears by the temple, swears by it and by Him who dwells in it. And he who swears by heaven, swears by the throne of God and by Him who sits on it" (Matthew 23:10, 22).

The Pharisees were well acquainted with God's law and knew that making an oath using God's name in vain was forbidden. They made debtors of the men who were under oath for their offerings. They didn't realize that they were putting the One who inhabits the temple and is seated on the throne in between. They did this without reverence.

"Woe to you, scribes and Pharisees, hypocrites! For you pay tithe of mint and anise and cummin, and have neglected the weightier matters of the law: justice and mercy and faith. These you ought to have done, without leaving the others undone" (Matthew 23:23).

They gave what was left over, alms and with that they tried to satisfy the law. They complied with a legal tithe, not understanding that the true law is love, as another mention of this passage in Luke 11 establishes.

"Blind guides, who strain out a gnat and swallow a camel!" (Matthew 23:24).

They were strict about others´ mistakes, attentive to the tiniest detail of the law, but they overlooked their own big faults.

"Woe to you, scribes and Pharisees, hypocrites! For you cleanse the outside of the cup and dish, but inside they are full of extortion and self-indulgence. Blind Pharisee, first cleanse the inside of the cup and dish, that the outside of them may be clean also" (Matthew 23:25-26).

Through their works, their impeccable garments, and the observance of the law, they hoped that their hearts too would be sanctified. They focused on appearance and through this, they hoped to be holy.

"Woe to you, scribes and Pharisees, hypocrites! For you are like whitewashed tombs which indeed appear beautiful outwardly, but inside are full of dead men's bones and all uncleanness" (Matthew 23:27).

They were the same as the beautiful and grandiose tombs they used. They did not show their actual condition, but instead, what they wanted to demand from others. But Jesus told them they were nothing more than dead bones. Obviously, bones have no life or spirit and are full of dirt.

"Even so you also outwardly appear righteous to men, but inside you are full of hypocrisy and lawlessness" (Matthew 23:28).

They showed their own righteousness through their confidence in themselves. They lived as if they didn't need God's justification because they believed they had obtained it by their own merits. They were righteous before men, but not before God. They were full of hypocrisy, falsehood, and iniquity, a wicked nature that they neither confessed nor cleansed themselves of.

"Woe to you, scribes and Pharisees, hypocrites! Because you build the tombs of the prophets and adorn the monuments of the righteous, and say, 'If we had lived in the days of our fathers, we would not have been partakers with them in the blood of the prophets.' 'Therefore you are witnesses against yourselves that you are sons of those who murdered the prophets'" (Matthew 23:29-31).

This same passage is repeated in the gospel of Luke, where Jesus tells them:

"Woe to you! For you build the tombs of the prophets, and your fathers killed them. In fact, you bear witness that you approve the deeds of your fathers; for they indeed killed them, and you build their tombs" (Luke 11: 47-48).

They certainly were not the ones who killed the prophets, yet they were filled with their fathers' wickedness. By justifying themselves before Jesus, He makes it clear that they were also complicit in the blood of the prophets. They were so hypocritical that they said, *"If we had lived in the days of our fathers..."* But they lived in the days of Jesus and crucified the Prophet of prophets. The very death of Jesus was promoted by them and shows that they were hypocrites, that they only demanded the shedding of innocent blood.

"Fill up, then, the measure of your fathers' guilt" (Matthew 23:32).

They were condemned just like their ancestors.

"Serpents, brood of vipers! How can you escape the condemnation of hell?" (Matthew 23:33).

The condemnation of hell is reserved for hypocrites. Scripture, when speaking of the coming of the Son of God, says:

"And will cut him in two and appoint him his portion with the hypocrites. There shall be weeping and gnashing of teeth" (Matthew 24:51).

The Word also says:

"Therefore, indeed, I send you prophets, wise men, and scribes: some of them you will kill and crucify, and some of them you will scourge in your synagogues and persecute from city to city" (Matthew 23:34).

Throughout all of Israel's history, they persecuted the prophets. What was the reason? The same they had against Jesus:

"The world cannot hate you, but it hates Me because ***I testify of it that its works are evil****"* (John 7: 7 author's emphasis).

"Jesus is a lover of truth; He taught the way of God truthfully and did not care about anyone›s opinion because He did not see men´s appearance" (Matthew 22:16, author's paraphrase).

These are the words of the Pharisees themselves and it certainly was true, for Jesus' ministry was based on truth, without any hypocrisy or intimidation. The Lord´s sinless life allowed Him to expose the lies in front of everyone because they had nothing to accuse Him of. They hated Him because He testified of their evil deeds.

" That on you may come all the righteous blood shed on the earth, from the blood of righteous Abel to the blood of Zechariah, son of Berechiah, whom you murdered between the temple and the altar" (Matthew 23:35).

A prophet flows in the gifts of revelation just like Jesus did. The best-kept secrets are revealed to them, which is why the scribes and Pharisees abhorred them. The authorities of the time wanted to corrupt the prophets, seeking statements in their favor. Because of hypocrisy, many ended up sweetening their words and flattering them. But Jesus was not one of these prophets. Neither were those who were righteous before God and whose courage was upright, since the Pharisees tried to kill them. Herod lived with Herodias, though she was his brother Philip´s wife. From the moment John the Baptist called him out on his sin, Herod tried to kill him. Hypocritical rulers do not want to have a righteous prophet around because they will call out all the filth they hide:

"O Jerusalem, Jerusalem, the one who kills the prophets and stones those who are sent to her! How often I wanted to gather your children together, as a hen gathers her chicks under her wings, but you were not willing!" (Matthew 23:37).

The Father's desire has always been to shelter His children under His shadow. But instead of repenting and allowing restoration, they were incited to stone those who were sent to them in the name of the Lord because of their hypocrisy.

Reaching God's glory implies honesty and sincerity, living out in the open, and dying to ourselves. Now, can you flow in the power of God and still be a hypocrite? The answer is yes! Many who don't have a healthy self-image are in ministry and move under the power of God, but do not obtain the glory of God. Because the Father's love for His people is so great, He allows those who serve Him to fulfill their assignment, including casting out demons, healing, and preaching the good news of salvation. However, as we´ve already covered, eternal condemnation is reserved for all who wear masks before men and God:

"Many will say to Me in that day, 'Lord, Lord, have we not prophesied in Your name, cast out demons in Your name, and done many wonders in Your name?'" (Matthew 7:22).

The reason Jesus tells them this is because of the hypocrisy, iniquity, and wickedness that were in their hearts. Apostle Peter carried out the ministry after having received the Holy Spirit and moved under the power of God, however:

"Now when Peter had come to Antioch, I withstood him to his face, because he was to be blamed; for before certain men came from James, he would eat with the Gentiles; but when they came, he withdrew and separated himself, fearing those who were of the circumcision. And the rest of the Jews also played the hypocrite with him, so that even Barnabas was carried away with their hypocrisy. But when I saw that they were not straightforward about the truth of the gospel, I said to Peter before them all, 'If you, being a Jew, live in the manner of Gentiles and not as the Jews, why do you compel Gentiles to live as Jews?'" (Galatians 2:11-14).

Reaching **God's glory** implies honesty and sincerity, living out in **the open, and dying to ourselves**

Look at the words of the apostle Paul, *"I withstood him to his face."* This is how we are to deal with hypocrisy. If something characterized Paul it was his honesty and because of it he made many enemies. Peter›s lack of identity stems from his *pretending*, in other words, he was acting. Furthermore, the power of intimidation not only made him fall into contradictions but also dragged down Barnabas. Paul says it was to be blamed, called out.

He also told him that he was not walking uprightly according to the truth of the gospel. This is what happens with hypocrisy: one lives behind a mask because of fear of lack of identity. Then, the servant of God ends up compromising the truth with the sole intention of being accepted, in other words, to avoid rejection.

On the other hand, Barnabas had become contaminated with this behavior. It was with this in mind that Jesus warned His disciples:

"In the meantime, when an innumerable multitude of people had gathered together, so that they trampled one another, He began to say to His disciples first of all, 'Beware of the leaven of the Pharisees, which is hypocrisy'" (Luke 12: 1).

Our Lord gave instructions about how to deal with hypocrisy because it contaminates others. Just a little of this yeast can leaven the whole dough, that is, just one person in authority who lives in a hypocritical way can contaminate and motivate many to behave the same, especially those who have no identity. As we saw in Galatians, it *drags others down*. Their intention is to keep hidden the truths about themselves and their lifestyle. However, the Word of God says:

"For there is nothing covered that will not be revealed, nor hidden that will not be known. Therefore whatever you have spoken in the dark will be heard in the light, and what you have spoken in the ear in inner rooms will be proclaimed on the housetops" (Luke 12:2-3).

Hypocrisy, like all of Satan's kingdom, is founded on a great big lie. Lack of honesty and sincerity results in condemnation unless you repent. It justifies you before men, but before God it condemns you. Furthermore, whether you are honest or not, that which you've so secretly treasured will be brought out by the light of the Word. And the shame will be more disgraceful than the glory that comes from repentance and confession. God does not demand perfection. He wants us to die to ourselves and wrap ourselves in His grace, showing ourselves as we are so that the glory may be His and not ours. The verse we just read uses the word *covered* because this is how hypocrisy is nested in the human heart; hiding, covering, and concealing.

Jesus treated the Gentiles, who did not know the law, with tenderness, forgiveness, and grace. However, with the Pharisees, scribes, and interpreters of the law, He was severe, like Paul was with Peter. You cannot have glory without death. What does fatherhood have to do with glory and orphanhood with hypocrisy? We know that Jesus Christ was an example in everything. So let's see how the identity He had as a Son led Him to glory. Let's read how He announced His death:

"But Jesus answered them, saying, 'The hour has come that the Son of Man should be glorified. Most assuredly, I say to you, unless a grain of wheat falls into the ground and dies, it remains alone; but if it dies, it produces much grain'" (John 12: 23-24).

Who is the grain of wheat? What does it mean to fall to the ground and die? You and I are the grain of wheat. In Jesus' case, in addition to dying to His will, He suffered physical death on the cross. For each one of us, dying means being naked before God and before men. It's to show ourselves as we really are; honestly, frankly, and dying to our own way of life. Losing our life is the only way to do the Father's will. It was not even easy for Jesus because they crucified Him. This was the anguish He felt prior:

"'Now My soul is troubled, and what shall I say? 'Father, save Me from this hour'? But for this purpose I came to this hour. Father, glorify Your name.' Then a voice came from heaven, saying, "I have both glorified it and will glorify it again'" (Matthew 12:27-28).

Jesus was afflicted in His soul. It must have been very intense for Him to know what was ahead of Him, though He knew He had been born to save the world and do His Father's will. He made sure to die in order to obey and glorify the Father in everything. The answer God gave to Jesus' request for the Father to be glorified was so beautiful, *"I have glorified Him."* How? Through all of the miracles His Son did on earth; every time that virtue came out of Him and every time it bore fruit. That is why the Father replied that He had already glorified His name and that He would do it again with Jesus' crucifixion, since this would be the greatest glory of all.

I imagine how pleased the Father was to see His Son obeying until death, even with a troubled soul. If He would have refused to die, today we could not be part of His abundant fruit. He had to fall to the ground, like the wheat, so that today you and I could enjoy salvation.

The heavenly Father will always be with us while we are dying to ourselves. He knows how painful it is. When the disciples left Jesus alone, He said, *"But I am not alone, because the Father is with me."*

This was Jesus´ confidence; He had His Father´s company even to face the moment of death.

"Jesus spoke these words, lifted up His eyes to heaven, and said: ´Father, the hour has come. Glorify Your Son, that Your Son also may glorify You´" (John 17:1).

"I have glorified You on the earth. I have finished the work which You have given Me to do. And now, O Father, glorify Me together with Yourself, with the glory which I had with You before the world was" (John 17:4-5).

Doing the Father's will glorified Him and Jesus. His obedience glorified the Father. The Savior would be glorified because He would return to His presence; Jesus would be back before His Father and in the glory He had before coming to earth. The same thing that happened with Jesus will happen with each one of us who have believed in Him. In Romans, we read that we have all fallen short of the glory of God.

Another way to say *falling short* is *destitute.* Adam and Eve were once *instituted* in Him, they dwelt in His glory in the Garden of Eden, talked with Him, and saw His glory in all its splendor. This is the reward of doing the Father's will.

Then, Jesus declares:

"And the glory which You gave Me I have given them, that they may be one just as We are one" (Matthew 17:22).

"Father, I desire that they also whom You gave Me may be with Me where I am, that they may behold My glory which You have given Me; for You loved Me before the foundation of the world" (Matthew 17:24).

Jesus cries out to the Father so that all who believe in Him would receive the same glory God gave Jesus and be in the same place the Father put Him for His mighty work of salvation. When Jesus´ time had come, before He was arrested, Peter tried to object and Jesus rebuked him:

"So Jesus said to Peter, ´Put your sword into the sheath. Shall I not drink the cup which My Father has given Me?´" (John 18:11).

What great determination Jesus had. He knew that He would drink the cup the Father had given Him, that He would die for humanity. But what is the cup the Father has given you? Are you also willing to drink it? Or do you seek glory without the cross?

We know that Jesus was crucified and rose again three days later for the Father's glory, as stated in Romans 6:4. Let us never be afraid of dying to give glory to God because just as He raised His Son, He will also do it with you.

Speaking of dying, I want to share the following testimony: I already shared that during my childhood I was looked down upon by my sisters. They were vengeful with me because of my father´s favor toward me. They rejected me because of the love I had received from him. But one of them, my youngest sister, was a tormenter. Because of her, I developed a lot of frustration within myself. She constantly scoffed at me and I didn't have the courage to stand up for myself. I was always persecuted by my older sisters; helpless, quiet, and lonely. I also cried a lot because of how they oppressed me.

I wish I would've been as patient as Joseph was with his brothers' attacks. But, by the time we became adults, I had all of these things bottled up in my heart. One day I decided to take matters into my own hands and take my younger sister's life. I thought that if she died I could live in peace. That thought ran around in my mind until I finally did it. I bought poison and tricked her into drinking it. They immediately rushed her to the hospital and called me to come see her, but no one knew what I had done.

I remember that when I saw her, her heart rate monitor read 85% and her eyes were large, her gaze was lost and she was in a coma. Looking at the scene, I fainted, and they had to revive me. So, without knowing God, I knelt on the ground, asked for His forgiveness, and begged Him to give my sister another chance.

Everything in me regretted what I had done. I felt hell itself had come upon me. The doctors told us to look for funeral services because she would not survive. Because they didn't know what kind of poison it was and because the quantity had been so large, they could not prescribe an antidote. I listened to the doctors talk, and although I knew exactly what poison it was, fear paralyzed me. So I kept silent and cried, asking God to give her another chance.

The next day, she came back to her senses and I offered to take care of her that night. She wore diapers and was in a deep state of hallucination; she yelled that she saw pink things in the room and that her throat hurt. The effect of the poison had wreaked havoc on her digestive system and the chance that she would survive with burns in her stomach was practically impossible to prevent. Her esophagus was burned because the poison went down her throat and into the emergency tubing. I saw my mom and all my sisters cry. It was a terrifying moment. But to God's glory, a few days later my sister left the hospital without any side effects, walking normally and with full mental faculties, as if nothing had happened to her.

When I converted to Christ, I confessed to my mother what I had done almost 10 years before. Nobody knew that I was the one who caused something so disastrous. I didn't have to fess up, but I had to be sincere and take responsibility for my actions. So after telling my mom, I told the people who restored me. However, I had not told my sister. I had an excellent relationship with her, I had discipled her, I had taught her the gospel of Christ. But every day I prayed to God and asked for the opportune moment to tell her the truth. Doing this is not easy, there´s the big temptation to just put on a mask. Furthermore, the devil whispered in my ear, "Now you´re a Christian, don't talk about that." Also, thinking about what people would say, what my older sisters would say, tried to stop me. They would think they were right about what they had always said about me. It would prove them right. But one day I got up early and God told me, "Today is the day; do it." So I went to my sister's house without justifying myself, without omitting any details, and I told her what I had done and asked her to forgive me. She cried a lot and after talking and praying, my sister hugged me and forgave me.

Maybe you haven't done something as serious as this or maybe you've done something worse that you wish had never happened. The truth is that God's grace has the ability to redeem the most abominable work of man. But there is a condition: dying to self.

We are being perfected as we die to the flesh, to our ego, and to what we believe about ourselves. When there is honesty, God is glorified. You cannot wait to receive the glory of God and to enter His presence with your face covered. You must expose yourself to His presence with truth, sincerity, and an unveiled face. What you do not confess the devil will; but when you are brave, the grace of the Father will accompany you and you will be like His Son Jesus Christ. He will give you the strength to face the cross and you will have the conviction that you are not alone.

I received a portion of His glory the day I confessed it to my mom, a bigger one the day I told my church mentors, and a new glory the day I told my sister. One day when I was ministering at church, there was a man to whom an "angel" had appeared in a dream. The "angel" told him that by not giving a message a person would die. That person died and he was terrified. Evidently, this was not an "angel" of light, but an unclean spirit disguised as an "angel." When I saw him terrified and crying because he and his wife would die, I felt God lead me to tell him this testimony. I was familiar with the empire of death, that is, I knew that only God rules over it. The "angel" told him that for not having done what he told him now his family would die.

I had done everything for my sister to die but that is not how the story ended. Then, I needed to tell him that the gates of death will not prevail against the Church. I knew what the devil had told him was a lie. But again, I had to die to myself, because telling him what I had done against my sister meant dying. But out of love for God's work and for the Father to be glorified, I told him. I remember his face, he looked at me extremely scared. I don't know what that represented for him, but for me, it was dying just a little bit more. That day I received another portion of His glory and today as I write this, I receive more. This is the naked grain that falls to the ground so that the glory is God´s by His grace. This is how we are exposed to justification by faith in Christ, not by our works because they are bad.

Identity gives you the courage to face anything. Knowing that the Father loves you, that He has forgiven you, that He has washed your filth with His blood, that His grace has redeemed you, that with His holiness He has justified you, allows you to enter His presence and present yourself before Him as an *approved worker that has nothing to be ashamed of and uses the word of truth well.*

The devil loses his power over you. He cannot accuse you before the throne of God and much less before men when through your confession, you have died to yourself. Satan cannot kill you twice, so when you are crucified with Jesus there is nothing he can accuse you of.

The Lord told King David that what he did in secret, his sons would do it in public and in broad daylight. These are the words that God, through the prophet Nathan, spoke to David for the sin he had committed and kept hidden:

" Why have you despised the commandment of the Lord, to do evil in His sight? You have killed Uriah the Hittite with the

sword; you have taken his wife to be your wife, and have killed him with the sword of the people of Ammon. Now therefore, the sword shall never depart from your house, because you have despised Me, and have taken the wife of Uriah the Hittite to be your wife.' Thus says the Lord: 'Behold, I will raise up adversity against you from your own house; and I will take your wives before your eyes and give them to your neighbor, and he shall lie with your wives in the sight of this sun." (2 Samuel 12:9-11).

"For you did it secretly, but I will do this thing before all Israel, before the sun'" (2 Samuel 9:12).

Is there really anything hidden from God? We see that the Lord knew all the details of the king's sin. Because of His omniscient and omnipresent character, God knows everything and is also everywhere, as Scripture says:

"For there is nothing hidden which will not be revealed, nor has anything been kept secret but that it should come to light" (Mark 4:22).

The same spiritual principle that exists for sin applies to honor since everything done in secret will be exposed to the light.

"But you, when you pray, go into your room, and when you have shut your door, pray to your Father who is in the secret place; and your Father who sees in secret will reward you openly" (Matthew 6: 6).

When you pray to the Father in secret, He will exalt you in public, for there is nothing hidden that should not be exposed to light. Everything that is secret will come to light because it is the same biblical principle, good or bad. The difference is that you voluntarily decide to die and expose yourself, if you don't, the enemy will. It is necessary to die:

"Foolish one, what you sow is not made alive unless it dies" (1 Corinthians 15:36).

"*It is sown in dishonor, it is raised in glory!*" (1 Corinthians 15:43a).

He who sows in dishonor is raised in glory. You must sow your disgrace and shame to be raised to glory because the heavenly Father´s conditions are not like those of this world. Notice that it does not say "sowing and reaping," but "sowing and made alive." This type of sowing is through death since only the dead can resurrect. Sowing shame is a way of dying, just like Jesus Christ received the Father's glory when He died on the cross.

Why is it so difficult to die? Because the human being is full of their own glory (pride); an empty glory full of vanity and personal works. A person decides how they want to appear before men, they choose the character and the mask they will wear according to the role they wish to embody. Clearly, that role isn't glory. We are all exposed before God for nothing is hidden in His light.

To glorify God you must first overcome orphanhood, fear, lies, slavery, condemnation, intimidation, and hypocrisy. All of these things try to stop a person from being glorified by the Father. Let us remember the Father's words to Jesus:

"For He received from God the Father honor and glory when such a voice came to Him from the Excellent Glory: 'This is My beloved Son, in whom I am well pleased'" (2 Peter 1:17).

The Son receives honor and glory from the place of glory, the presence of the Father. First, He calls Him *Son*, affirming His fatherhood over Him. Then, He calls Him *beloved.* An orphan can never receive these words from the Father if fatherhood is not revealed to them. Additionally, it is important to understand that God is not angry with us.

On the contrary, we are loved by Him. Understanding these truths and obeying the Father, make Him delight in His children because they glorify His name. And so, the Father is glorified in His child and the Father glorifies the child as a reward. When you no longer live in pride, everything you do will glorify your Father's name and this will be your glory.

We will live like this:

"Therefore, whether you eat or drink, or whatever you do, do all to the glory of God" (1 Corinthians 10:31).

Apostle Paul also declares:

"Foolish one, what you sow is not made alive unless it dies" (1 Corinthians 15:36).

We must decrease, die to our ego and way of life, and voluntarily surrender our life as Jesus Christ did. We cannot be a seed that bears fruit for the glory of the Father without dying. Only then will we be brought to life.

"And what you sow, you do not sow that body that shall be, but mere grain—perhaps wheat or some other grain. But God gives it a body as He pleases, and to each seed its own body!" (1 Corinthians 15: 37-38).

That nakedness (sincerity) that we sow before the Father is what He covers with His grace and power. We are the vessels where He wants to deposit and show His glory in such a way that the glory is His and not ours. He is the One who gives fruit to the grain you sow, He is the One who glorifies it and Who gives each person a portion of His glory.

"There is one glory of the sun, another glory of the moon, and another glory of the stars; for one star differs from another star in glory" (1 Corinthians 15:41).

Everyone carries a different weight of glory depending on what they have sown through their willingness to die, that is, surrender their life through death. It is not men who glorify, but the Father.

Jesus said:

"I do not receive honor from men" (John 5:41).

"How can you believe, who receive honor from one another, and do not seek the honor that comes from the only God?" (John 5:44).

"It is sown in dishonor, it is raised in glory. It is sown in weakness, it is raised in power" (1 Corinthians 15:43).

Stripping yourself and probably exposing yourself to the dishonor of many in order to do the will of the Father will make you rise in glory. And what is sown in weakness will rise in power, for we also read that the power of God is perfected in the weakness of the human being. So when I am weak, then I am strong through Him. But the first step is the struggle with your ego to expose your shame and weakness. We must cast off the sin that beset us:

"Therefore, laying aside all malice, all deceit, hypocrisy, envy, and all evil speaking, as newborn babes, desire the pure milk of the word, that you may grow thereby" (1 Peter 2:1-2).

Now, let's read the words of the apostle Paul:

"Do we begin again to commend ourselves? Or do we need, as some others, epistles of commendation to you or letters of commendation from you? You are our epistle written in our hearts, known and read by all men; clearly you are an epistle of Christ, ministered by us, written not with ink but by the Spirit of the living God, not on tablets of stone but on tablets of flesh, that is, of the heart" (2 Corinthians 3:1-3).

We are open letters ready to be read, in which there is nothing hidden, shameful, hypocritical, or any lie. Rather we bear witness with our lives because we are sincere, as the Scripture says.

The word sincere comes from ancient Greece where wax masks were used in theaters. When the actors took them off, they became people without masks, that is, authentic. This explanation of sincere is simply a popular etymology generally recognized by linguists. At the time, letters were also sent with a wax seal to prevent the messenger from reading them. When they were sent without wax, these letters could be read by everyone. In the same way, sincere children of God are open letters ready to be read.

As open letters ready to be read, we are accredited to men by the Father, that is, we do not need the recommendation of men. The Holy Spirit will do it as He did with Jesus Christ:

"I am One who bears witness of Myself, and the Father who sent Me bears witness of Me" (John 8:18).

Paul adds:

"Therefore, since we have such hope, we use great boldness of speech" (2 Corinthians 3:12).

Paul confronted Peter without a mask, which is with boldness of speech and an unveiled face.

"Now the Lord is the Spirit; and where the Spirit of the Lord

is, there is liberty. But we all, with unveiled face, beholding as in a mirror the glory of the Lord, are being transformed into the same image from glory to glory, just as by the Spirit of the Lord" (2 Corinthians 3:17-18).

We will look at the Lord's face without masks or supporting roles, but humble, meek, and with unveiled faces, as in a mirror. We will see our face through Him and be transformed with a greater weight of glory every time through His Spirit, just as Moses´ face shone because of the glory in the Father's presence. We will look into that mirror and instead of seeing our own life, we will see Him.

Our conscience plays a leading role in seeing the glory of God:

"This being so, I myself always strive to have a conscience without offense toward God and men" (Acts 24:16).

These words give us a very important spiritual key so that the glory of God can be reflected in a person's life. You must have a conscience at peace with God and with men. This speaks of confessing, dying to ego, forgiving, and many other conditions. But above all, dying to one's personal lifestyle and giving way to the will of the Father. Why would a man like Paul, who had been a murderer, practically a terrorist and a hitman, say that he tried to have this kind of conscience?

"Then Paul, looking earnestly at the council, said, ´Men and brethren, I have lived in all good conscience before God until this day´" (Acts 23:1).

I insist: how could a man with Paul´s track record say about himself with such certainty that he lived before God with a good conscience? This is what redemption through Jesus Christ does, justify us before God. People who have done really bad things are generally trapped in their consciences; laden with guilt and condemnation. The pressure of others to find out about their past often leads them to live hypocritically. It is the lack of identity in Christ that makes some people hide their most shameful memories. But there is no glory covering sin. The glory is God's because He restores us when we expose ourselves to personal death through confession. The glory is of the Father and not ours. God will not deposit His glory in a hypocritical vessel, since a vessel in that condition would be filled with pride before himself and others, and the Lord does not share His glory with anyone.

It is for this reason that the person must die before God and men in order to be trustworthy before the Father. Now, only sons and daughters can do this. Only those who are sure of their identity like Jesus was, Who died and was glorified in addition to glorifying the Father. The apostle Paul did not take the merits for himself, because a man like him needed all of God's grace to be justified. But that same grace that was granted to Paul is available to all who want to die.

"I tell the truth in Christ, I am not lying, my conscience also bearing me witness in the Holy Spirit" (Romans 9:1).

This conscience allowed him to live in communion with the Holy Spirit and lead a life of integrity before Him.

What was this apostle´s service like?

" I thank God, whom I serve with a pure conscience, as my forefathers did, as without ceasing I remember you in my prayers night and day" (2 Timothy 1: 3).

He didn't serve with a *clear conscience* because he had never sinned, but because he was as close to God's grace as possible. With these words, Paul defends himself in front of kings and people of the social elite of that time, and he does so with great dignity. Because of the grace he received, he gave declarations like this:

"But from those who seemed to be something—whatever they were, it makes no difference to me; God [a]shows personal favoritism to no man—for those who seemed to be something added nothing to me" (Galatians 2:6).

What a great truth. The Father does not care who you´ve been, He has the grace to elevate you to a holy priesthood based solely on the merits of the blood of Jesus Christ. In the verse that follows the one we just read, Paul says that he has been given the grace to be an apostle after having been a murderer.

There is no **glory** without a cross,
there is no cross **without death!**

Before ascending and being crowned in glory, Jesus showed Thomas His scars. If you want to receive glory from the heavenly Father, you must be willing to die to yourself and show your scars. Thomas was Jesus´ most unbelieving disciple. There are many, who like Thomas, will only believe if you are able to show what God has done in you as a living testimony.

As soon as we are empty of ourselves, naked, exposed, and with nothing to boast of, then we are fit to receive the glory that comes from the Father; when we look at His face without anything to be ashamed of or accused of. The moment when there is nothing left of ourselves in front of the mirror we will see ourselves in Him.

Glory is the manifestation of the presence of God reflected on your face, just like when Moses´ face shone as he exposed himself to the face of the Lord. He did not have to say that he had been with the Lord because his face reflected the glory of the Father. This glory carries with it the power of God so that His presence is evident in your life and manifested in those around you. Like when you are under the sun with your face uncovered, without sunblock, a sun hat, or a mask; it is not necessary to say that you were in the sun because it will be obvious to everyone.

Glory is something reserved only for sons and daughters! The child prefers to die if an act of obedience glorifies their Father.

Orphans, on the contrary, seek their own glory. They do not do God's will, but their own. They are always frustrated because they do not fulfill the purpose for which they were created. They do not know their assignment within creation, they are merely actors who live pretending.

Jesus didn't receive glory from men nor did He seek His own glory, as we have already seen. Seeking your own glory is not glory, for this is a blessing that only God can give.

Glory is, then, the manifestation of the **presence of God** reflected in your face

Glory weighs upon a life, it is the very presence of God manifested in and through a life.

Let's see the Hebrew meaning of the word *glory*:

Kabód; rarely. Prop. Weight, but only figuratively speaking. In a good sense, splendor or abundance, flower, glory, glorify, glorious, honor, honorable, to give honor, majesty, noble, power, wealth, lavishness (*Spanish Strong Concordance 3519 y 3513*).

This word comes from the word *Kabéd*, whose meaning is: Primary root; feeling the weight, in a bad sense (heavy, severe, obtuse) or in a good sense (numerous, rich, honorable); cause to be heavier in the same two senses; overwhelm, accumulate, aggravate, increase, cause, blind, give, distinguished, harden, esteem, force, glory, glorify, glorious, burdensome, honor, honorable, honored, glorious, illustrious, distinguished, boast, annoyance, multiply, noble, heavy, to weigh, renamed, rich, cover, old age, venerate (*Spanish Strong Concordance 3513*).

As you can see, all the meanings of this word are the reasons why pride is so sought after. Everyone wants to be illustrious, rich, honored, distinguished, but few want to die. That is why its first meaning is seldom because very few people are willing to die. In all of these definitions are the characteristics of the hypocrites whom Jesus Christ confronted. Everything they were after is covetable. I can say with total clarity that hypocrisy is the anti-design of glory because it produces false results (pride) and this really isn't glory, it is an antagonism of the true glorification that comes when we do the will of God.

Glory is the destiny for the children of God, that is, to return to the Father! To the place and relationship that He prepared before the foundation of the world: destiny. And if we do become something, it is because of the grace of God.

"But by the grace of God I am what I am" (1 Corinthians 15: 10a).

Prayer to receive God's Fatherhood and Glory

(Hypocrisy)

Father, I come before You to ask Your favor so that the pride of life does not cloud my mind; so that pride does not darken my understanding and distance me from your truth; so that at all times you show me the true intention of my heart and through your power, I can maintain a clear conscience before You and men. Teach me to die to myself, join me as I saw my shame and give me the courage to do it.

My God, may I always walk face to face, without hypocrisy, without lies, without manipulating the truth to hide my true condition because by doing so I put up an obstacle that prevents the manifestation of Your glory in my life.

I ask forgiveness for all the times that I have behaved falsely and I renounce this behavior in my life, I renounce the spirit of lies, I renounce pretense, I renounce hypocrisy and I renounce vainglory.

Help me to cleanse myself of the old yeast so that I may be a new dough, unleavened as I should be. Take away the old leaven of malice and wickedness from me and make me like unleavened bread, that is, sincere and authentic.

Do not allow me to be a stumbling block that drags others towards hypocrisy for fear of losing the glory of men that is worth nothing and is nothing compared to the glory that comes from You.

Thank You for helping me obey Your will and bring glory to Your name.

All this I ask of You in the name that is above all, Jesus the Savior. Thank You, my God and my Father, because I know that I have asked according to Your will and that You will grant it to me because I trust in You.
Amen.

First Testimony:
From Orphanhood to Having the Identity of Being A Child of God

This is the testimony of a 58-year-old man, who is the eighth child among ten siblings, all from the same father and the same mother. He grew up in a humble family. His mother was a self-sacrificing woman completely dedicated to her home. She made her living ironing other people's clothes and doing everything she could from home to work and at the same time take care of her children. This was not an easy chore since they were a large family. When this man told me about her, I perceived in my spirit that she was a woman with a character like Abigail´s, Nabal's wife, who later became King David´s wife. A lady with a personality like Scripture describes her, *"of good understanding and beautiful appearance."* When witnessing her behavior in light of her husband's abuse, King David said, *"Blessed is your advice."*

The truth is that this man´s mother was submissive to her husband. However, they had many problems because he got home drunk and beat her horribly in front of all their children for no apparent reason. He was motivated by uncontrollable anger that he carried within himself. It was easy to let all that anger out on this type of woman since she did not complain or defend herself. Everyone in his family was paralyzed with fear in front of him because he was abusive and violent.

From his healing process, I remember one of his stories that really made my heart ache:

One day, like any other day in his family, his father came home drunk. He trained horses and after his work day, he brought the horse home. He mounted this animal straight into the living room. Seated on the horse, he took the mother by the hair and beat her without any compassion. This son who deeply loved his mother watched, paralyzed with fear, from a corner of the house. He watched how this man mistreated the person who had given him life, his greatest love; the woman he admired because of her efforts to support him and brothers every day; that woman who never complained, who was not offensive or sarcastic in light of her husband's abuse and who, on the contrary, endured everything in silence. That day, while he was telling me about this episode in his life, his eyes were like crystals that held back many tears. He spoke with strength but he was like a child closed in on himself; a scared and sad little boy. I held back my own tears as I sensed the nobility of his wounded heart and could see how orphanhood had brewed deep within his being. While this child witnessed such an evil act, he was completely violated inside, as if he had been assaulted in the identity of his manhood. Even though he loved his mother, he could not defend her from her aggressor because that man was bigger, stronger, and his father. The person who was supposed to love him and protect him. This is how the wound of orphanhood takes hold of a human being, through humiliation, abuse and mistreatment, as the feeling of forsakenness grows to agony.

Then, when he was 11 years old, his mother died of a fatal heart attack on a Sunday morning on the floor of a Catholic church. That day, he had gone to church with his younger brother, who was only five years old. The news confirmed that his mother had died and because she was the only support in this family, the whole unit fell apart. The siblings split up, but this 11-year-old boy was left completely alone with no source of love and no one to protect him. As he roamed the streets, he worked in anything he could to earn his food and daily shelter. I imagine that over and over, he asked himself, *"Where is God?"* How can a person believe in divine fatherhood if the only fatherhood he knew had ruined his life...

He was an exemplary son who loved his mother and helped in everything he could to ease her heavy load. From a very young age he was agile and diligent. For example, he grew lettuce in his house and sold it in the market. One day, with the money he saved from these sales, he bought her a berry-colored dress. I imagine the joy in the heart of this mother when she received that gift from her young son. She was buried with that same dress; such a painful image that would never be erased from this son's mind. The love of his life had died; the only person who had ever expressed love to him. He was left in complete solitude.Time passed and with a lot of effort he became a professional, a prestigious lawyer, a cultured and respectable man. However, the wounds in his soul were intact. Sometimes he exploded in anger, he was tough, strict, highly distrustful, fearful and his soul was still that of that wounded child. But on the outside, he showed himself as a strong, arrogant and intellectual man who tried to forget the past, as if all this had never happened and as if the pain did not exist.

He had known Jesus Christ as his Savior and Lord for 13 years, but he did not have a relationship with the heavenly Father, since the wound caused by his biological father prevented him from approaching and seeing God as a Father. For him, a father figure never provoked tenderness, protection or love.

For months we talked about the Scriptures, until the day chosen by God to talk about Orphanhood arrived. His eyes filled with tears as he remembered and recounted his childhood. Although it was not easy because he was uncommunicative and I was a stranger, I am sure that God honored this man's faith. His faith was unshakeable, for he knew that God was real because he had accompanied him in his moments of loneliness. The revelation of God's fatherhood reached him; we did a study and when he finished he said to me, "Yes, I feel like an orphan." This statement was the only thing our God needed to work in him. That day, while we were praying, he renounced fear, mistrust, orphanhood, anger, and injustice. He reconciled himself to the memory of his biological father, forgave him for all the harm he caused him, his mother, and all of his siblings. Before this day, he had seen his father and forgiveness bloomed in their hearts toward each other. Because of this attitude I also believe that the truth about the fatherhood of God was revealed to him. We cried out for Jesus Christ to reveal the Father and we asked for the adoption that God has promised in the Holy Scriptures.

This man has a 35-year-old son whom he had not seen for four years. The relationship between them was broken, but by receiving God's forgiveness and reconciliation from Him as His son, he extended it to his own son. He had never called him son but that day he called him son and said, "Forgive me, I was an orphan and that's why I couldn't be a father to you." I heard the conversation from the lower floor of the house and, after they reconciled, I heard the beautiful and enthusiastic voice of a girl, around eight years old, who said to him, "Grandpa, I am your granddaughter!" He didn't know her, but it was evident that she was expecting to meet him soon. This is the manifestation of the glory of God and the strength that fatherhood brings with it; family restoration of all generations.

Second Testimony: From Heartbreak to the Father´s Perfect Love

The Lord sent me to Houston, Texas. I attended Lakewood Church, where I was invited to a prayer group. There was a young woman there, very pretty, with a sweet yet withdrawn look. At the end of the meeting, she asked for prayer for her job since she was having problems with it. I prayed for her request and then she approached me and told me that she wanted to invite me to lunch. Of course, I accepted the invitation because I know that the Lord does everything for a purpose. Before leaving the house where I was staying in Houston, I prayed for her and asked the Father what He wanted to do in the life of this woman. While I was praying, I had a vision. I saw a girl, about five years old, sitting on the ground leaning on her knees and looking down. There was a man standing there who clapped his hands over her and seemed to intimidate her. Then the Lord brought these three words to mind: shame, fear, and intimidation. At that moment, I received an impression in my spirit about the seal of God's love and a gold necklace of great value which would remove the shame. I didn't understand anything but I was sure that she would.

"Set me as a seal upon your heart, as a seal upon your arm; For love is as strong as death" (Song of Solomon 8:6a).

The time came and she picked me up for lunch. When we were riding in the car, I told her, "Forget lunch, I have to tell you something that the Lord showed me today in a vision." When I told her what I had seen, she was visibly upset and said, *"I've never told anyone, not even my mother knows. That girl you saw is me and the man is my father, he abused me since I was little."* Her eyes filled with tears and mine too. I could feel the affliction she had kept in her heart all her life. People like her who suffer painful experiences like these are excessively distrustful due to the obvious fact that she could not trust her own father. Helping someone with this wound requires a genuine intervention from the Holy Spirit to prompt them to accept the help. She had been in the Christian church for many years so she knew the gospel, however, no one knew of the pain that she carried in her soul.

We did not have lunch but instead headed to the church parking lot. There I told her, "If you want to open your heart, the Holy Spirit is here to take away all the pain that you have in your soul." She accepted and we began to pray.

She cried a lot and I felt like there was a person gagged up inside her who wanted to scream but couldn't.

Fear paralyzed her because she was in a spiritual prison. It was a prison where that girl was terrified, petrified by fear; she was alone, completely stripped, and violated. Then, I understood why the Lord had told me those three words and told me to tell her, "My love is like a seal on her arm, on her chest. Put a gold necklace on her neck, which will make her hold her head up high like someone who wears a jewel of great value on her neck because there will never be shame in her again. She will never lower her head and thus My love will be displayed in her." How would a woman walk when she wears the love of God represented on a necklace on her chest? With her head held high! She will never be ashamed looking down. The jail door had been opened.

""The Spirit of the Lord is upon Me, because He has anointed Me to preach the gospel to the poor; ***He has sent Me to heal the brokenhearted, to proclaim liberty to the captives*** *and recovery of sight to the blind, to set at liberty those who are oppressed"* (Luke 4:18 author´s emphasis).

All of that unfair and evil work was redeemed by God on that day.

"He who sins is of the devil, for the devil has sinned from the beginning. For this purpose the Son of God was manifested, that He might destroy the works of the devil" (1 John 3:8).

This scene was similar to when Joseph was taken out of jail and they put a gold necklace around his neck because he was no longer a prisoner but a free man.

" Then Pharaoh took his signet ring off his hand and put it on Joseph's hand; and he clothed him in garments of fine linen and ***put a gold chain around his neck****"* (Genesis 41:42 author´s emphasis).

It is very hard when a woman feels ashamed of herself. She had suffered toxic relationships in which men had abused her even physically. She longed to be loved, her soul was thirsty for love, since her father, who should´ve been the source of love, had made her an insecure and lacking person. However, she was now loved by the heavenly Father.

"He brought me to the banqueting house, ***and his banner over me was love****"* (Song of Solomon 2:4 author´s emphasis).

Just a couple of days after this experience of freedom, my time in Houston ended. I believe that God works at the exact moment and when we least expect it.

Third Testimony:
From Slavery to the Freedom of Being A Child of God

I had arrived in the city of Bogota and wanted to attend the church, *El Lugar de Su Presencia* (The Place of His Presence). A 60-year-old lady who lived in the same building where I was staying, offered to take me. Apparently, she thought I did not know the Gospel and she wanted to be kind by taking a possibly new believer to church. She paid for the taxi and wouldn't let me do it. She was so kind to me, the way a believer treats someone who is not yet a believer. I know that all of this is seen by the Lord to work in a person's heart. While this was happening, I asked the Father, "What do you have for her, what do you want to do in her life?" As we watched the service, I continued to meditate. When we came back, the Holy Spirit said to me, "Tell her the testimony of the rape." I was shocked because I did not know this lady. I had only known her for two hours and she was quiet and reserved. She spoke to me as if I did not know the Word of God because she really thought that I didn't know anything about the Lord. So I only listened to her until I interrupted her and told her what God was telling me. Then, I shared a testimony about sexual abuse in which God had glorified Himself. She was silent and froze as if paralyzed. When we arrived at our destination, she said to me, "Could you come to my house tomorrow morning at ten?" "Yes," I replied.

The next day at 9:59 am I rang the doorbell of her house. When she opened the door she told me, "I have been praying and asking the Lord if you are the right person to tell what I have kept in my heart. It is something that I have never shared. So I asked God for a sign. If you came without me having to call and arrived on time, then it would be an answer for me. At 9:59 you knocked on the door! I also decided to fast for the Lord for 21 days and today is my seventh day, I believe that you are the one I have been waiting for." I was surprised.

She began to tell me that when she was 15 she had been abused and that she had not been able to forgive that person. The Lord reminded her that she still had a wound in her soul. She told me that when she was six years old, her father and mother died. Her older sister deceived her by telling her that she would take her for a walk when the truth was that she took her to an orphanage. She cried in a corner all day because she felt completely alone and confused.

Apparently, the nuns said her behavior was normal since all the girls that were left there reacted the same way. She was in that place from the ages of six to fifteen.

The food was, in her words, disgusting. They served them rotten chicken and meat; the vegetables and food on the plate had worms, and everything smelled awful.

The nuns were strict and unforgiving, and they treated the girls extremely harshly. She remembers the day they punished her by locking her in a bathroom where there was no sink or anything else. It was just a cold ceramic room. Although they locked her there without a blanket or pillow, one of the nuns had compassion on her and when she turned off the lights she gave her a blanket without the others knowing. Before five in the morning, she came to take the blanket, without letting anyone notice that she had spent the night with her. She was also locked in dark rooms and constantly cried. She suffered greatly while locked up in that place; unprotected, enduring humiliations, harassment, and the recurring thought that she was not worthy of love because she had been abandoned in that place and completely forsaken.

She then returned to the topic of what that man had done to her, it was her older sister´s husband. He blackmailed her with that abusive and lewd behavior. She was 15 years old but since she had grown up in an orphanage with nuns she was an innocent teenager, naive and deprived of the things that happen in the world. This man took advantage of all that to keep her as a prisoner. She allowed all of that because she had nowhere to go; she endured all of that harassment for the sake of having shelter and a place to live.

Although she was now a 60-year-old woman, she still suffered the consequences of all these traumas because she was still the innocent, six-year-old girl who was abandoned in an orphanage. She has daughters but they didn't understand their mother´s strange behaviors because they did not know her story. Due to everything she kept in her soul, this woman had a severe problem in her digestive system. She threw up everything she ate and could not tolerate food. Food disgusted her because she remembered and imagined the food at the orphanage.

She also had serious rejection problems towards herself, despite being a beautiful woman with blue eyes and beautiful skin. She told me that she didn't even want to wash her face because she thought her appearance was horrible. She was ashamed of herself and cried for hours in front of the mirror, believing that she was ugly. Satan's works in this life were devastating, as he had distorted her image, especially the way God saw her. On the other hand, there was her state of health.

She had a disease in her bones, her walking was slow, stiff, somewhat stooped, and her knee was weak. So when she finished recounting her testimony, I shared this word with her:

"When I kept silent, my bones grew old through my groaning all the day long" (Psalm 32:3).

Hiding sin is a very serious matter for the bones. They get old and lose mobility when trying to resist pain. She did not understand why if this man was the one who had attacked her, she had to suffer the consequences. But as long as she was silent and did not remove all this from her soul, Satan was still tormenting her.

"For day and night Your hand was heavy upon me; my vitality was turned into the drought of summer. I acknowledged my sin to You, and my iniquity I have not hidden. I said, 'I will confess my transgressions to the Lord,' and You forgave the iniquity of my sin" (Psalm 32:4-5).

Then I explained the trap of unforgiveness and we read the parable of The Two Debtors.

"Therefore the kingdom of heaven is like a certain king who wanted to settle accounts with his servants. And when he had begun to settle accounts, one was brought to him who owed him ten thousand talents. But as he was not able to pay, his master commanded that he be sold, with his wife and children and all that he had, and that payment be made. The servant therefore fell down before him, saying, 'Master, have patience with me, and I will pay you all.' Then the master of that servant was moved with compassion, released him, and forgave him the debt. But that servant went out and found one of his fellow servants who owed him a hundred denarii; and he laid hands on him and took him by the throat, saying, 'Pay me what you owe!' So his fellow servant fell down [a]at his feet and begged him, saying, 'Have patience with me, and I will pay you all.' And he would not, but went and threw him into prison till he should pay the debt. So when his fellow servants saw what had been done, they were very grieved, and came and told their master all that had been done. Then his master, after he had called him, said to him, 'You wicked servant! I forgave you all that debt because you begged me. Should you not also have had compassion on your fellow servant, just as I had pity on you?' And his master was angry, and delivered

him to the torturers until he should pay all that was due to him. So My heavenly Father also will do to you if each of you, from his heart, does not forgive his brother his trespasses'" (Matthew 18:23-35).

This is the trap behind unforgiveness. The wounded heart cannot understand why, if it has been the victim of something so disastrous, it would remain in a spiritual prison if it does not forgive. For this reason, Satan binds with resentment and locks the person in a spiritual prison. He confines that part of the soul in a jail that is guarded by an executioner. On the other hand, the heavenly Father, even with all His love for us, cannot go against Himself. There are spiritual laws that He has designed, *"Forgive us our debts, as we forgive our debtors."* God›s forgiveness occurs in the same measure as I grant forgiveness to others.

That day, she confessed everything that was in her heart to the Father; the resentment and bitterness she felt against this man, and the brokenness of her soul for suffering such a painful childhood. She forgave her abuser with all her heart as well as all the people who had mistreated and offended her. As she did that, I saw within me the dark room that she had described to me.

There, her soul was confined to loneliness, isolation, and fear. We cried out to Jesus Christ, the only One who can undo the works of the devil, to enter that dark room and get this girl out of jail. She moaned and cried and sobbed; it was like reliving all her pain but the Holy Spirit comforted her.

She would never be alone again, for now, she knew she

was not an orphan because she had a Father who loved her and had come to her rescue.

"And they shall call them The Holy People, The Redeemed of the Lord; And you shall be called Sought Out, A City Not Forsaken" (Isaiah 62:12).

Conclusion

What is the destination of our pilgrimage on earth? In the words of Jesus, speaking about Himself, this is the answer:

"Jesus said to him, 'I am the way, the truth, and the life. No one comes to the Father except through Me'" (John 14:6).

Christ is the way that leads us to the Father and the Father is our destination at the end of the road in our heavenly home. One day, we will close our eyes and the living soul will leave our body. At that moment, we will be brought before God Almighty. When we open our eyes, we will be in front of Him and live in His presence for all eternity. Then, everything we have done on earth will make sense. However, it is not necessary to die to enjoy the presence of the heavenly Father. It is possible to enjoy it now through Christ, who redeemed us with His blood and ended the separation that came as a result of orphanhood and forsakenness.

The agony of not having a place of refuge will fade. Perhaps you have never known a family, but in Christ it is possible to have one and, not just any family, but the Royal family. For this reason, fix your gaze on the One who loved you. Forget vanity and resentment, and receive this promise by faith:

"*I will never leave you nor forsake you*" (Hebrews 13:5b).

If you have not had a stable home, let go of all the weight and pain. Allow Jesus to grant you the revelation of the heavenly Father. Don´t get caught up in the feelings that bind you and take you captive; fix your eyes on things above, not on things on earth. The time you have here is short, but the time you will live with the Father will be eternal.

The home you have dreamed of is in God. Christ came to reveal the Father and then returned to heaven to prepare a place for us:

"*In My Father's house are many mansions; if it were not so, I would have told you. I go to prepare a place for you*" (John 14:2).

What will that dwelling that Christ went to prepare for us to be like?

Scripture says it´s beautiful. It is a city, the heavenly Jerusalem with walls made of jasper. It has been built with pure gold, similar to clear glass, adorned with precious stones such as sapphires, agates, emeralds, chrysolites, beryl, topaz, chrysoprase, hyacinth and amateurs. It has pearl doors, all in pure gold, transparent like glass. There is no need for the sun or moon to shine because the glory of the Father illuminates it. The Lamb will be its light, therefore there will be no need for a lamp. There will never be darkness in this city because it will never be night. What a wonderful place! For its rivers of living water are like crystal. There, suffering will end because there will be no more curse and the throne of God and the Lamb will be in the middle of it. Can you imagine what that place will be like? Filled with angels adoring God in harmony. Where the corruptible will clothe themself with incorruption. A place that cannot inherit flesh or blood. A place where we will go without anything earthly, not even our own body.

By all these truths we understand the apostle Paul when he said that dying was gain for him. This is the reason why Scripture affirms that we´ve been freed from the fear of death, because when the day of departure comes there will be no fear and it will be the most glorious moment that we will experience. We will not die, but will live and go to the Father's house. We will return to Him and our heavenly home and have eternal rest.

In that place, all tears will be wiped away, there will be no death, there will be no more crying or weeping or pain because the former things have passed. It is useless to hold onto the pain and resentment because you will not be able to take it to your Father's house.

And if you manage to let go of the weight, your reward will be this:

"He who overcomes shall inherit all things, and I will be his God and he shall be My son" (Revelation 21:7).

This is where we really belong. This is our home, our family and this will be our final destination. In this house, you are truly welcome, the Father will be waiting for you with open arms. You will be in front of Him like a child no matter how old you are, you will see the Father you always dreamed of, you will have the welcome you have always longed for. It won't be necessary for you to wear anything to please Him or earn His love, for you have always been loved by Him.

" For now we see in a mirror, dimly, but then face to face. Now I know in part, but then I shall know just as I also am known" (1 Corinthians 13:12).

Before that day, you will have seen the Father through the mirror of His Word. But at that moment, you will see Him face to face and you will come to know how you were created in the intimacy of His love.

"I will not leave you orphans;
I will come to you"
(John 14:18).

Upcoming book,
in the editing workshop

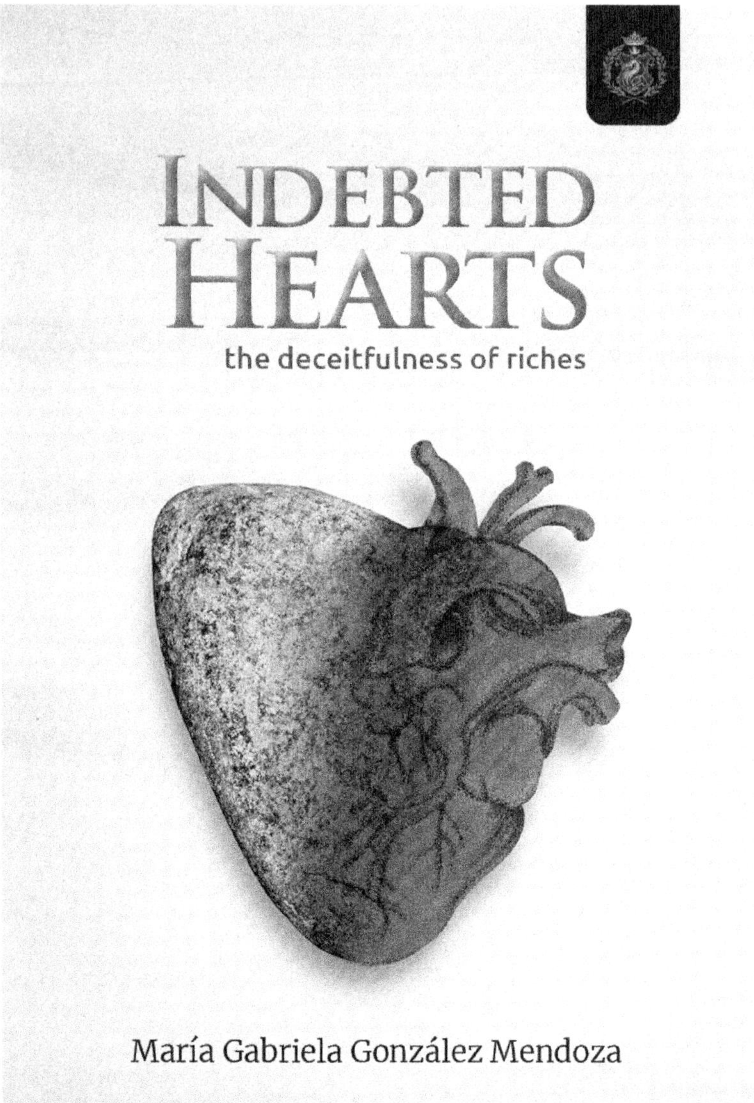